Black and Minority Ethnic Voluntary and Community Organisations

Black and Minority Ethnic Voluntary and Community Organisations

Their role and future development in England and Wales

Mike McLeod, David Owen and Chris Khamis

Policy Studies Institute
London

UNIVERSITY OF WESTMINSTER

PSI is a wholly owned subsidiary of the University of Westminster

The Joseph Rowntree Foundation has supported this project as part of its programme of research and innovative development projects, which it hopes will be of value to policy makers, practitioners and service users. The facts presented and views expressed in this report are, however, those of the authors and not necessarily those of the Foundation.

Published for the Joseph Rowntree Foundation by the Policy Studies Institute

A CIP catalogue record for this book is available from the British Library.

ISBN 0 85374 778 4
PSI Report No. 869

Typeset by PCS Mapping & DTP, Newcastle upon Tyne
Printed by

For further information contact
Policy Studies Institute, 100 Park Village East, London NW1 3SR
Tel: (020) 7468 0468 Fax: (020) 7468 2201 Email: pubs@psi.org.uk
www.psi.org.uk

Contents

List of tables and figures

List of acronyms and abbreviations

BMEO	Black and minority ethnic organisation
BME	Black and minority ethnic
BRN	Black Regeneration Network
BTEG	Black Training and Enterprise Group
BVSC	Birmingham Voluntary Service Council
CAB	Citizens' Advice Bureau
CAN	Community Action Network
CEMVO	Council of Ethnic Minority Voluntary Organisations
DTI	Department for Trade and Industry
DoE	Department of Education (now Department for Education and Employment)
ERDF	European Regional Development Fund
ESF	European Social Fund
HART	Handsworth Area Regeneration Trust
HES	Handsworth Employment Scheme
LLSC	Local Learning Skills Council
LOVAS	Local voluntary activity surveys (produced by Home Office)
NCVO	National Council for Voluntary Organisations
NLCB	National Lottery Charities Board
PQASSO	Practical Quality Assurance System for Small Organisations
RSL	Registered Social Landlord
SLA	Service Level Agreement
SRB	Single Regeneration Budget
TEC	Training Enterprise Council

Authors' note: definition of black and minority ethnic

The term black and minority ethnic is used by the Home Office, Commission for Racial Equality and other official bodies dealing with race and ethnicity issues. Black and minority ethnic organisations have been defined, for the purposes of this report, as organisations primarily led by persons of black or minority ethnic origins and primarily serving these communities. Black and minority ethnic is used in this report to cover 'visible' (non-white) minorities, excluding other ethnic minorities such as those of Eastern European origin.

Acknowledgements

The Centre for Research in Ethnic Relations at Warwick University and CSR Partnership, a Birmingham-based regeneration and economic development consultancy, would like to thank the following:

- Danielle Walker and Pat Kneen of the Joseph Rowntree Foundation, who provided much support, many insights and general guidance throughout the research.
- The Advisory Group, who provided many useful comments in connection with the definition of terms and the interpretation of findings: Cathy Pharoah (Charities Aid Foundation); David Reardon (Social Exclusion Unit); Dipali Chandra (Cadbury Barrow Trust); Aziz Tharani; Jeremy Crook (Black Training and Enterprise Group); Amir Bhatia (Council of Ethnic Minority Voluntary Organisations); Jean Foster (Home Office); Tony Marshall (advisor to the Home Office); Steve Pittam (Joseph Rowntree Charitable Trust); Vandna Gohil; and Samantha Rennie (National Lotteries Charities Board).
- Brenda Addison and Asad Rehman of CSR, who helped interview mainstream and community agencies.
- Edgar Hassan, who was responsible for organising the community fieldwork, and researchers: Maureen Millbourne; Laurent Media (who also assisted with data analysis); Ranjit Senghera (who helped supervise the Handsworth fieldwork); Adela Anthony; Fazila Jogiyat; Andrew Togobo; John Ssekkono; Rena Grewal; Rugiatu Wurie; Nkechi Oburota; Ochucko Grace; Yaa Chenewa Addo; Christina Skerritt; Santokh Singh Gill; Ricard Moren; Marcia Burroughs; Donna Thompson; and Tony Bennett.
- Anne Shaw and Jas Bains of the Centre for Research in Ethnic Relations, who provided key input in compiling the database, structuring the survey and analysing the results.
- BTEG, Project Fullemploy, SIA, BRN, Runnymede Trust, the 1990 Trust, Brent Indian Association, Asra Housing Association, and other organisations (including the Arts Council, local authorities and libraries), who provided BMEO contact details.
- The staff of mainstream agencies in Birmingham and Brent who gave up a significant amount of their scarce time to discuss issues concerning black and minority ethnic organisations.
- Lynn Eaton, who edited the final report.
- And, particularly, all the black and minority ethnic organisations who took part in the survey, and discussion groups.

As always, the Centre for Research in Ethnic Relations and CSR Partnership accept full responsibility for the interpretation of the information and views provided by all the above.

Executive Summary

1. Introduction and background

This chapter looks at the development of black and minority ethnic organisations in England and Wales and why they are in the spotlight so much today. In particular it touches on the impact of the MacPherson report into the handling of Stephen Lawrence's murder.

It sets out the objectives of the research, which were: to map the sector; look at links with mainstream funders; and consider how the sector might develop.

The chapter considers how changes in funding, with the shift away from funds earmarked for black and minority ethnic organisations and introduction of a 'contract culture', have affected the sector. It voices concern that a specific black voluntary sector could be squeezed out unless its role is specifically acknowledged by mainstream funders.

The authors outline the methods used in the research – a postal survey and two case studies – and the limitations of the study, which did not include religious organisations, because of their entirely different funding base. They also acknowledge that the operations of black housing associations, which have a larger than average funding base for the sector (though still small compared to all voluntary organisations in England and Wales) significantly affect the overall picture of black and minority ethnic organisations.

2. Black and minority ethnic organisations and their role in the community

This chapter provides a brief history of black and minority ethnic organisations in England and Wales from the early part of the 1900s.

Based on the postal survey, it looks at their position today. The data include the numbers and geographical distribution of these organisations; a description of their legal status and governance arrangements; and an analysis of their main activities and services and of the users of their services. The authors also look at the question of whether there is a distinct black voluntary sector.

This section contains the evidence from the survey of individual residents in the two case study areas.

3. The resource base

This chapter covers the resources and funding of the organisations surveyed. The survey is used to discuss the sustainability, growth constraints and development needs of BMEOs, as perceived by the groups themselves.

In order to get a clearer picture of the issues facing different parts of the black and minority ethnic sector, the researchers have grouped responses into different bands, based on annual income. They look at main funding sources and how they differ for each group. They also look at how the legal status of organisations differs and how both this and funding levels affect the type of people they employ, the services they provide, and the number of volunteers and type of property they make use of.

This chapter also looks at the importance of providing BMEOs with sufficient support for them to develop.

4. Relationship to mainstream agencies

This looks at the relationship with mainstream agencies and the perceptions of these agencies of the role and development needs of black and minority ethnic voluntary organisations.

It reports on the interviews with mainstream agencies in the two case study areas and outlines some of the more successful partnership arrangements. It highlights concerns expressed by BMEOs at the changing funding arrangements and their potential impact on the organisations. Finally, it states that there is not much evidence of rigorous monitoring or evaluation of BMEOs as organisations with a specific capacity to meet community needs.

5. Conclusions and policy implications

This chapter assesses the direction of public policy and practice, its strengths and shortcomings. It states that BMEOs have an important role to play in reducing social exclusion and that they have more staying power than previously recognised.

However, they need help and support if they are to develop to meet the needs of the next generation. It suggests ways this might be achieved. The importance of religious organisations within black and minority ethnic communities must be acknowledged and should be included in grant programmes.

The move towards a 'contract culture' and lack of a strategic policy towards BMEOs may undermine their work, the researchers argue. But with appropriate support and funding, the sector could be made sustainable – and help address the problems associated with social exclusion.

Summary of Conclusions and Recommendations

Overview

- BMEOs are an integral part of the infrastructure required for eliminating social exclusion and deprivation. This fact needs to be embedded across the whole vista of social, economic and environmental policy. The ultimate aim should be to eliminate the social exclusion experienced by many in the BME communities.
- The existing Voluntary Sector Compact framework could be extended to encourage local mainstream agencies to ring-fence resources specifically for BMEO capacity building as part of their planning/consultation budgets, and as part of their service delivery budgets.
- The Home Office initiative (Grants to Strengthen Black and Minority Ethnic Infrastructure Organisations, 1999) to establish regional support networks for BMEOs should continue and be extended.
- BMEOs have more staying power than the common perception suggests. However, reinforcing sustainability has to be a fundamental part of any policy for strengthening BMEOs and is an essential ingredient of capacity building for the minority ethnic communities as a whole.
- A positive move would be the establishment of a network of BMEO mentors by the Home Office, which could act as an agent of change throughout public and voluntary institutions.
- What is needed is far more strategic coordination of support to BMEOs at appropriate geographical levels, to ensure that they receive funding packages which improve their long-term sustainability and the quality of services they can provide.
- The role of BMEOs in any 'joined-up' area strategy should be recognised and clearly defined, so that they too can approach issues and their target groups more holistically. Many of these organisations are already providing services and advocacy across a range of policy areas and could therefore provide a good foundation for developing a more joined-up approach.
- 'Breaking down of the silos' is recognised as a policy objective by government departments in tackling social exclusion. It now needs to be reflected in policy and practice towards BMEOs (and the voluntary/community sector more generally) at a regional and more local level. This will require a review of policy and practice by each wing of central, regional and local government, by quasi-public agencies and by large voluntary organisations which examines their overall impact on social exclusion and racial equality.

- Responsiveness to local differences is significantly enhanced by having, and listening to, local 'patch' workers, and by employing BME staff.
- The long-term sustainability of BMEOs will depend on the extent to which resources are made directly available to them, so that they can continue to provide services to the immediate community. The extent to which 'neighbourhood targeting' forms part of the government's strategy for dealing with social exclusion and deprivation will therefore be of prime importance to BMEO survival.
- BMEOs with a well-established local base will need to become increasingly involved in alliances and partnerships with non-BMEO bodies. A key issue will revolve around the allocation of resources via these alliances, with BMEOs demanding the resources which will allow them to play a significant role, while remaining viable.
- Flexibility will be need to be exercised in drawing in BMEOs into area-targeted initiatives. Although BMEOs tend to focus their activities on specific localities, reflecting neighbourhood concentrations of BME residents, our survey suggests that these localities will tend to be larger than some of the areas currently targeted.
- Grant programmes need to be operated with sufficient flexibility if the important role BME religious organisations play in the secular life of BME communities is to be supported.
- Programmes which include aims of delivering benefits to BME communities should be monitored for the achievement of these aims. They should include qualitative indicators of whether these benefits are likely to be sustainable.
- Mainstream organisations have to find ways of helping innovative projects to 'graduate' into more long-term, mainstream funding and support, such as providing shared premises and mentoring support from more established BMEOs, help in making contacts, and championing the initiatives in partnership forums.

Conclusion

Black and minority ethnic communities continue to face deprivation, social exclusion and discrimination to a greater extent than many other communities in England and Wales, and mainstream organisations are failing to tackle these issues adequately. This has been recognised in the Stephen Lawrence Inquiry and in the emerging government policies on social exclusion and neighbourhood renewal.

However, if this recognition is to lead to effective policy and practice – and to real change – then measures to support and sustain black and minority ethnic voluntary organisations need to be given a much more prominent and central role.

These measures need to be implemented in a coordinated, strategic and long-term way. It would be better to encourage agencies to develop their own services, and to introduce measures to ensure their sustainability, rather than continuing with the current fragmented and contract driven arrangements.

The alternative is the persistence of a vicious cycle of social exclusion.

1. Introduction and Background

Why the study was commissioned

There has been an increasing interest in the role of black and minority ethnic-led voluntary and community organisations (BMEOs) in recent years – although the existence of British black and minority ethnic organisations is by no means a new phenomenon. Nonetheless, if this part of the voluntary sector is to survive and grow, it has to adapt to meet the needs of the second, third and forthcoming generations of black and minority ethnic groups.

'Ethnic' associations were first established before the First World War in the maritime industries and in the port cities. Following the large scale migrations from the Indian sub-continent and the Caribbean in the late 1950s, immigrant associations emerged in every main centre of settlement, particularly in connection with the need to find work and accommodation – and often in the face of racism and exclusion. (See page 11 for a fuller description of the origins of the 'black voluntary sector'.)

Our initial research shows that currently, there could be as many as 5500 BMEOs operating in England and Wales. Contrary to common perception, not all of these are based in inner cities.

An increasing number are based in provincial towns and cities where relatively large numbers of people from ethnic minority groups are found.

Despite their long existence in the UK, there has previously been little investigation into the role of BMEOs in Britain. Recent interest in these organisations is probably a reflection of three factors:

1. Growing recognition in public policy of the importance of the voluntary and community sector in general (for example, the Home Office sponsored Voluntary Sector Compact and the weight given to community involvement in many regeneration initiatives).
2. The Macpherson report on the Stephen Lawrence Inquiry, which placed the issues of racial discrimination and institutional racism back on the national agenda.
3. Lobbying by black and minority ethnic umbrella organisations.

This mapping report, funded by the Joseph Rowntree Foundation, sets out to find out about and record what services are currently offered by the sector, where its funding comes from, and to look at the position of the BMEOs within the voluntary sector. It concentrates on 'visible' minority ethnic groups. Groups such as Jews, Poles, Italians, Cypriots etc are not included.

The report does not comment (other than anecdotally) on the standard of service provided, nor give direct comparisons with white voluntary organisations. No doubt many of the comments made by members of the community about the services on offer from BMEOs or the way they are managed could as easily apply to white-run voluntary organisations. However, there is no equivalent study of white voluntary organisations with which to make any comparisons.

The main objectives of the study were:

- To determine the general distribution of BMEOs in relation to the distribution of the ethnic minority population; to identify the type of services they provide to the community; and to highlight gaps or under-provision in these services, both geographically and on the basis of potential demand.
- To assess the type, nature and strength of existing links between BMEOs and providers of financial, technical and other resources.
- To identify the key factors that influence the level, nature and sustainability of support to these organisations as a whole.
- To assess the current robustness and sustainability of the BMEO sector and the principal factors affecting this.

As far as we are aware, this is the first national study of the black and minority ethnic voluntary and community sector.

Context

Deprivation and social exclusion

The role and significance of black and minority ethnic organisations needs to be placed in the context of social exclusion and poverty.

Of course, not all minority ethnic communities would be considered disadvantaged. For example, Modood, Berthoud et al[1] state that:

> *Chinese people and African Asians have reached a position of broad parity with the white population – behind on some indicators perhaps, but ahead on others. It would not be appropriate to describe them as disadvantaged groups.*

But, although some black and minority ethnic groups, such as East Africans, may have reached parity with the white population, they may still suffer from racial discrimination. And on almost any index of social exclusion, certain ethnic minority communities will figure disproportionately.

Defining social disadvantage is fraught with difficulties. The circumstances leading to this outcome are complex and include class, background, employment opportunities, kinship patterns, cultural traditions, residential location, educational experience and institutional racism. But if we look at factors such as income and

Table 1 *Households below half the national average income (percentage)*

White	28
Caribbean	41
Indian	45
Pakistani	82
Bangladeshi	84

Source: Ethnic Minorities in Britain, Modood & Berthoud, 1997, PSI

employment, the differences are clear. According to Modood, Berthoud et al, while only 28 per cent of white households earn below half the national average income, for Bangladeshis the figure is 84 per cent (see Table 1).

Unemployment rates for ethnic minorities as a whole between June 1995 and 1996 were twice as high as for white people. For some minority groups, for example African and Bangladeshi men, they were over three or four times as high,[2] and in some areas, such as London, the unemployment rate reaches an astonishing level (more than 60 per cent of young black males are unemployed).

This is not just an issue of economic deprivation, but of multiple deprivation. Individuals from certain minority ethnic communities are much more likely to be imprisoned, excluded from schools, diagnosed with a mental illness, to suffer from particular types of illness, crime and poor housing conditions.[3] In addition, all minority ethnic groups experience racial discrimination and racist harassment, particularly where families are isolated outside of familiar networks.[4]

Deprivation tends to be concentrated in specific geographical areas or neighbourhoods. Analyses of the family resources surveys have found that minority ethnic groups are generally located in low income areas and are generally resident in areas of high unemployment.[5] More than half of Britain's African Caribbeans and Africans, and more than a third of South Asians, live in districts with the highest rates of unemployment.

People who live in certain inner city areas, such as Handsworth in Birmingham or Stonebridge in Brent, tend to suffer from multiple deprivation – higher unemployment, discrimination in finding jobs, low incomes when they find jobs, poorer health, higher crime and dereliction in the surrounding environment. All these facets of deprivation tend to reinforce each other, creating real difficulties in helping people out of their poverty, and requiring 'joined-up' solutions. This is the fundamental point made by the government's Social Exclusion Unit in their draft strategy for neighbourhood renewal.

Our study sought to look at the extent to which BMEOs addressed, or helped others to address, issues of deprivation and social exclusion, and to measure the geographical base or coverage of these organisations.

Sources of funding for BMEOs

An underlying theme of this study is an assessment of the importance of different sources of funding to minority ethnic-led groups, the nature of this funding and its impact on their sustainability.

Government funding

In the 1970s and early 1980s, local authorities became important funders of BMEOs. However, cutbacks in local authority spending were an increasingly common feature of the later 1980s and 1990s. Many white-led voluntary organisations suffered as well as BMEOs. But BMEOs were doubly hit by a change in the way funding from central government was allocated.

There is a widespread perception that funding became increasingly related to economic development and regeneration, channelled through special funding regimes. For example, the single regeneration budget (SRB), introduced in 1994, highlights the way that money is channelled through special funding regimes. Funds from a variety of sources (the Home Office, DTI, DoE etc) were pooled to create a single 'pot', with an emphasis on economic regeneration.

This was particularly important for BMEOs, as Home Office funds formerly earmarked specifically for assisting ethnic minority communities were thrown into the 'pot' without there being a requirement that they continue to benefit those communities.

The general experience of BMEOs with the SRB provides an illuminating illustration of the main issue:

> *Black communities were directly and severely affected by the introduction of the SRB because all of the grants traditionally targeted at black communities were put into the SRB. These included most of Section 11, the ethnic minority grant and the ethnic minority business initiative. Combined with the phasing out of the urban programme, and the difficulty black groups have in gaining any sustainable access to a broader range of funding sources from the public sector, the impact on black communities was devastating.*[6]

In recent years, funding regimes have tended to emphasise a strategic, 'joined-up' approach, based on partnership between the public, private and voluntary/community sectors, and often involving targeting of particularly deprived geographical areas. Given the concentration of ethnic minorities in deprived areas and their greater likelihood of experiencing multiple deprivation, it could be argued that these developments might provide a better funding environment for the groups covered by this study.

However, the exact opposite appears to have happened. There has been a decline in statutory funding available for black and minority ethnic groups, including that from local authorities. During the 1980s, the 'contract culture' emerged, with its emphasis on professionalism, service level agreements, output measurement, and 'quality assurance'. This gave rise to a feeling among these organisations (confirmed by the evidence collected in this study) that access to resources was being severely eroded under the new funding regimes (including European funding).

Their general view is that the 'contract culture' has tended to put BMEOs at a disadvantage – a view no doubt shared by small white voluntary organisations, although we have not collected comparative data in this study to support this view.

BMEOs, however, have (with exceptions) neither the historical and organisational links of white-led voluntary organisations, nor the organisational structure or experience to negotiate their way successfully through the new contract regime. There is some evidence that smaller, less formalised organisations are often unable to meet 'contract culture' criteria. They also face new standards imposed by managers who are forced to rationalise limited funds, and who offer an 'across-the-board' approach, where everyone gets the same treatment.

Larger voluntary organisations, who have the clout to develop more formulaic approaches, tend to do much better on 'contract compliance', by having 'proper' accounting procedures, service standards, management systems, business plans and relatively generous levels of administrative resources. Smaller organisations have had to compete in other ways – through their accessibility and flexibility, alongside a personal relationship with users.

In the case of black voluntary organisations, these issues are magnified. Asylum seekers/immigrants, for example, constitute a sizeable fraction of the beneficiaries. The need for 'people sensitive' services (addressing language barriers, feelings of isolation, respect for culture, racist hostility etc) is paramount. Established ethnic minority residents of the areas in which the newly arrived immigrants have settled are able to act as 'go-betweens'. They can develop fairly close personal relationships with the new arrivals, while being reasonably confident in representing their needs to the agencies with which they have had past dealings.

These 'old hands', however, are still only partially integrated into the institutional and administrative networks representing the 'service delivery' mechanisms of the state sector. They are still struggling with the issues of employment barriers, educational marginalisation, linguistic and cultural exclusion, residential segregation and racist harassment. They face even more formidable challenges than white-led community organisations in establishing alliances and partnerships for change.

Research suggests that partnerships that have successfully bid for funding rarely have any black representation, although there was often representation from a mainstream voluntary sector umbrella group (according to the National Council of Voluntary Organisations-funded Black Training and Enterprise Group and the Local Government Information Unit's report *Race and Regeneration*).

Charitable funding

Charitable trusts and foundations are seen as alternative sources of funding for BMEOs. More than half of the groups taking part in our study had experienced statutory funding cuts and had often been advised by statutory agencies to apply to trusts and charities for funds. This had created a sudden increase in the number of minority ethnic applications to this source.

The amount of funding flowing to the black and minority ethnic-led groups from charitable sources was investigated by studies carried out in 1990 and 1999.[7] These found that:

- In 1990 trusts allocated, on average, less that 1.4 per cent of their funds to black groups. The 1999 study suggests this has risen to 3 per cent.
- Grants were fairly small, tending to be around £5000, although there was a handful of large grants, according to the 1999 study.
- Most of the grants in the 1990 study came from a small core of funders active in the field of social justice.

The more recent study also showed that most grants 'tended to be towards social care or civil society, law and advocacy activities' and were 'most prominent in London'.

- A significant proportion of funders showed no awareness of racial disadvantage, with overwhelming support for a 'colour blind' approach. More than 80 per cent of funders in the 1990 study believed that ethnic minority status should be disregarded when considering applications.

The 1990 report recommended that a specialist distribution agency with contacts in the black voluntary sector be established to distribute block grants on behalf of other funders. This is an idea that has been recently revived by the Council of Ethnic Minority Voluntary Organisations (CEMVO), a national minority ethnic umbrella organisation. CEMVO has been seeking to establish a grant-making trust which will pool the resources of government agencies, trusts and foundations, and individual members of the minority communities (who will be asked to make a regular financial donation) to ensure that 'dedicated' funding is available to BMEOs.

Over the last few years, minority ethnic-led groups have also had the opportunity to access resources provided by the National Lottery Charities Board (NLCB), which has taken steps to ensure that they are fairly represented as fund recipients. Similarly, the Charities Aid

Foundation has ring-fenced funds for specific use by these groups, and the Millennium Commission is 'unofficially' aiming to do the same.

Figures are generally not yet available on the proportion of funds from these sources going to black-led groups, although the NLCB has just started to monitor this (results should be available by 2002). The NLCB has monitored the proportion of its funds which address issues of deprivation (55 per cent) but has only recently begun monitoring the proportion that goes to black-led groups. Figures are not available nationally for funding to BMEOs from other sources, such as from local authorities, which remain major funders despite funding reductions. Our research suggests that very few have begun the monitoring required to collate such figures.

Is there a specific black voluntary sector?

A closely related policy issue is whether the needs of BMEOs should be seen as any different from those of other voluntary or community organisations. For example, the Deakin Commission on the Future of the Voluntary Sector[8] reported:

... comments on the particular contribution of black and ethnic minority organisations centred mainly on their ability to offer a significantly different perspective from mainstream organisations, or to provide service geared to the needs of particular communities. A few respondents took a different

approach. Network Housing and Care, and the Rainer Foundation, while recognising that there are some advantages to black-led organisations providing their own services, felt that fully integrated services are preferable. ADEPT in Coventry felt that the contribution of black and ethnic minority organisations is sometimes over-stated – while they provide a useful representative function, users are more interested in the quality of a service than its auspices. LVSC asked whether black organisations really are very different from the rest of the sector, and suggested that the 'myth of separateness' needs questioning.

SIA, a now defunct BMEO national umbrella body, was emphatic in its submission to government on the Voluntary Sector Compact that the 'black voluntary sector' was indeed distinct:

The black voluntary sector is firmly of the view that a dualistic approach is necessary to further relations between the government and the sector... there should be a separate compact to address the needs of the black voluntary sector... A 'black compact'... [outlining] the expectations of the relationship between the black voluntary sector and its working partners.[9]

The underlying argument here is a political one. If the intentions towards, and expectations of, the black voluntary sector are not clearly spelt out to those allocating funds, then the black voluntary sector will be squeezed out of the process of policy development and service delivery, rather than becoming more deeply involved.

This debate is related to the potential role that 'infrastructure organisations' could play at both regional and local levels in determining the fate of BMEO funding.

Approach to the study

The methods used for carrying out the study included an initial postal survey of BMEOs throughout England and Wales, followed by case studies in two areas of high concentration of minority ethnic communities. These were the Soho and Handsworth areas of Birmingham and the Alperton and Stonebridge areas of Brent in London.

The postal survey received 200 responses and included questions on:

- purpose, length in existence, legal status and governance;
- services provided and beneficiaries;
- physical and human resources, including volunteers; and
- growth constraints.

Further details of the survey are provided in Chapter 2.

The case studies (also detailed in Chapter 2) were undertaken to obtain the type of qualitative information that cannot be obtained from postal surveys. While they provide a more in-depth picture of two smaller areas, caution is needed in generalising their results to a

national level. However, they do provide evidence which can act as a counter-check to any biases that are unavoidable in postal surveys.

The case studies involved three components:

1. Interviews with individual members of minority ethnic communities resident in Birmingham and London. These covered their perceptions of organisations active in their area and the needs they hoped they would serve. The interviews were partly held in local shopping centres and partly door-to-door.
2. Individual and focus group discussions with representatives from BMEOs in the two areas, covering their roles and needs, in particular their needs to secure sustainability.
3. In-depth interviews with key mainstream agencies (including voluntary agencies) providing support to organisations in the two case study areas. These focused on the nature of this support, including resource flows, and perceptions of the role and sustainability of these organisations.

Limitations of the study

It was decided from the outset to exclude explicitly religious organisations. This was based on the perception held by many funders who provide resources to the voluntary sector that religious organisations, such as churches, temples and mosques, have quite different kinds of resources, connections and purposes from other voluntary sector organisations. It was felt that if we were going to look at the resources that sustain the voluntary sector, it might distort the experiences of other BMEOs, whose funding and experiences were very different.

However, although the research did not actively include religious organisations (unless they were running a group clearly aimed at secular, as opposed to spiritual, community benefit), the study reveals that black communities themselves conceive of the voluntary sector in terms of their church or mosque group. This carries a strong message for mainstream funders such as local and central government and Lottery Fund distributors: if they are serious about involving the black voluntary sector, religious organisations must be considered an important element, not actively excluded as at present.

The picture which emerges from the postal survey is more complex than the stereotyped view held by some people of BMEOs as small and poorly funded. The sector was revealed as encompassing organisations ranging from the tiny, with incomes under £10,000 per year, to housing associations with annual incomes of several million pounds.

Some of the characteristics of different parts of the sector are illustrated in Chapter 3. For example, characteristics of small, non-formal groups (most of whom have funding of less than £50,000 a year) are compared with those who have formal legal status (who are more

likely to have incomes of £100,000 a year or more).

The fact that a large number of housing associations, with large resources, responded to our survey may well have presented a different overall picture of the sector from the one many people might have been expecting.

Again there is a message for funders from this research: that BMEOs are not a homogeneous group. They may share similar concerns about funding or their future development, but there are many different types of voluntary organisation, as there are in the white voluntary sector.

Relationship to other studies

Defining the voluntary sector and classifying the types of organisation to be found within it is no easy task.[10] The most current, widely used, international classification is based on a series of studies carried out by Johns Hopkins University.[11] We used this system to identify the broad areas of activity in which BMEOs might be involved. The roots of many of these organisations lie in Africa, the Caribbean or in South East Asia, and we felt it might eventually be of some interest to compare these organisations with their NGO counterparts in the 'countries of origin'.

At the same time, we wanted to get some idea of how the subjects of our study compared with other UK-based voluntary organisations. For this purpose, we found the local voluntary activity surveys (LOVAS), carried out under the auspices of the Home Office, to be the most useful.

Voluntary activities in the UK are very broad in scope. They range from the work of large national charities, such as Shelter, Oxfam or Save the Children, through to the activities of local communities trying to improve their residential circumstances, down through the vast number of individual 'carers' who are helping the sick, elderly, and disabled.[12] The LOVAS survey provides a method for classifying this wide range of activities – allowing for comparison between different subsectors of the voluntary sector as a whole. In particular, it distinguishes between voluntary organisations (which work 'on behalf of others') and community organisations (which work 'on behalf of ourselves and people like us'). This helped us think through whether the organisations we were surveying fell into either category or both, which was important because of the common perception that BMEOs are, essentially, loosely structured 'community groups'.

The LOVAS survey also provided a good point of comparison because it gives a detailed overview of voluntary and community sector activities in at least some parts of the UK and includes useful data on black and minority ethnic involvement in the voluntary sector.

Unfortunately, only one or two of the areas covered by the two LOVAS surveys to date have a significant minority ethnic population. Smethwick was the only area with which we could make any sort of useful comparison. Compared with the rest of the country, Smethwick ranks highly, not only on volunteering levels, but on income, overall increase in income, number of funding sources per organisations, and relationships with other organisations. The percentage of organisations belonging to parent or umbrella bodies is, however, low.

2. Black and Minority Ethnic Organisations and Their Role in the Community

Origins of the 'black voluntary sector'

The existence of the British BMEO is by no means a recent phenomenon. Before the First World War, 'ethnic' associations were common in the maritime industries and port cities. These associations, which included the 'Sons of Africa' in Cardiff, the African Progress Union in Liverpool, and several organisations serving Sylheti seamen in London, were focused primarily on sickness and distress relief, and on 'arranging meetings on matters of interest'.

Following the large-scale migrations from the Indian subcontinent and the Caribbean in the late 1950s, immigrant associations emerged in every main centre of settlement, particularly in connection with the need to find work and accommodation – often in the face of racism and exclusion.

As 'New Commonwealth'[13] immigrant communities found themselves unable to access mainstream services, they organised alternative methods for meeting their needs. Informal credit groups, for example, were set up for the purpose of home purchase or for starting a business in the face of indifference on the part of banks and building societies. Similarly, supplementary education schemes were established as a reaction to the mainstream practice of placing black children in the lowest streams of the education system.

Both Asians and African Caribbeans took to pooling their savings until they were sizeable enough to purchase property. The Asians operated through an extended family system or 'mortgage clubs' and bought short lease property which they would rent out to their kinsfolk and countrymen, Similarly the West Indians operated a 'pardner' (Jamaican) or 'Sou-Sou' (Trinidadian) system... it was a sort of primitive banking system engendered by tradition and enforced by racial discrimination...[14]

Self-help therefore developed out of the necessity of meeting unmet needs. Support extended not just to family and friends but to those in the community who are in a similar position.[15]

In other cases, the impetus for the growth of associations came from political or workers' groups which, drawing on post-colonial and black American struggles, started providing information, education and advocacy services to the community. They were often closely connected with campaigns against racial attacks, immigration controls and/or discriminatory policing practices. They helped to mobilise these socially excluded communities in obtaining rights, benefits and access to services which were otherwise being denied them. BME strikers in the 1960s, for example, were often Asians, whose only support came from local organisations and communities. The temples gave free food to the strikers, the grocers extended credit and the landlords waived the rent. At the national level, organisations such as the Indian Workers Association and the Institute for Race Relations were established.

By this time, following the arrival of families from the countries of heritage, religious institutions – churches, mosques and temples – were beginning to be established. These played an active role in fostering community cohesion and family welfare. Access to the 'welfare state' services available to the wider host community, however, proved a challenge to immigrant families.

Black and minority ethnic organisations began to deal with almost every facet of the ethnic minority interface with mainstream service providers. In the main areas of ethnic minority settlement, they were increasingly called on to provide:

...general advice and information on various issues such as health care, housing, benefits, immigration, racial harassment, translation and interpretation and education... [or]... services with a direct care element such as day care for children and elderly, luncheon clubs, homes, family and community centres, drop in centres for people with mental health problems.[16]

BMEOs thus originally arose to deal with a number of issues connected with the settlement of New Commonwealth citizens in the UK. John Rex summed up the different roles they played as follows:

Immigrant associations had four major functions, namely, overcoming social isolation, affirming values and beliefs, doing social and pastoral work for their clients, and acting as quasi-unions defending the interests of their members. The first two of these functions are clearly concerned with sustaining the community; the third is partly a communal and partly an associational function; only the fourth is clearly associational.[17]

Maintaining group identity and providing for the welfare of the community were clearly core functions of emerging BMEOs. On the one hand, BMEOs have played a direct communal role in maintaining group (religious and cultural) identity, in promoting group welfare, and in sustaining the community as 'community'. On the other, they have performed an advocacy function – challenging the wider society to recognise the needs and rights of ethnic minorities. Our survey results confirm that this thread continues to run through their present-day activities.

It is evident that community self-help was an important foundation for the emergence of BMEOs:

Self help... developed out of the necessity of meeting unmet needs. Support extended not just to family and friends but to those in the community who are in a similar position.[18]

But it is also evident that the state has long recognised the need to engage with the question of the 'non-provision' of basic services to minority ethnic communities. This began with the early efforts by the Home Office to support organisations which 'offer practical help to immigrants' and was later reflected in successive waves of urban initiatives. However, although this approach encouraged the initial development of BMEOs, it was not so successful in ensuring their long-term sustainability.

In the wake of the Stephen Lawrence Inquiry, it is evident that both the community-oriented (helping maintain community identity) and state-oriented (service delivery) aspects of the BMEO role need to be taken into account.

Given the realities of institutional racism and the changing demographic patterns of both minority and majority ethnic communities, the sustainability of BMEOs will primarily depend on two things:

1. continuing to maintain a sense of identity and cultural cohesion among those they serve; and
2. simultaneously providing access to the full range of services and rights, supposedly available to all UK citizens.

One of the principal aims of our work was to establish what sort of shape BMEOs are in to achieve these tasks.

The postal survey

The sampling frame for our postal survey was created by compiling a database of BMEOs in the areas of greatest ethnic minority populations in England and Wales. We compiled a database of some 4000 groups through contacts with local authorities, community relations councils, minority ethnic groups themselves, health authorities, arts councils and other bodies.

The database was inevitably biased towards groups which have achieved a measure of public funding. There were also gaps in some geographical areas, and gaps resulting from the exclusion of religious organisations from the survey. Nevertheless, the database was sufficiently large and comprehensive to allow a representative survey to be undertaken.

The distribution of organisations in the database broadly mirrored the minority population distribution of England and Wales – the majority falling within the areas of greatest density, from London to the Manchester/Leeds and Midlands (especially Birmingham and Leicester) conurbations. Significant numbers were also located in other parts of the Midlands (especially Birmingham and Leicester), the Pennine towns, and the cities and towns of South East England, such as Luton, Reading, Oxford and Peterborough.

Following a protracted process of trying to eliminate groups which were defunct, or had moved, we selected, at random, 1000 BMEOs from the database and sent them a questionnaire.

We received 200 replies, a response rate of 20 per cent, which is about the average for a postal survey of this type. However, the questionnaire sent out was quite long and requested fairly detailed financial information, which may have deterred some organisations from completing it, especially those which were smaller, less well-resourced or more recently established.

The response rate was highest in the northern region, Wales and Inner London, and lowest in the South West, the North West and Greater Manchester. The response rates also tended to be high in more rural and more suburban districts, and lower in the major population concentrations.

We have no hard evidence to explain why there was such a variation in responses. Probably the main factor was the quality of the directory information used in compiling the list of organisations. In some cases it may have been out of date or dominated by organisations associated with particular council departments or programmes.

There might also be an element of 'survey fatigue' for organisations located in major cities, while those organisations located in the suburbs and rural areas may have been surveyed less frequently.

The diagrams below depict the geographical distribution of organisations in our database (Figure 1) and the distribution of the organisations which responded to the survey (Figure 2). Although far from a perfect match, it does indicate that the coverage has been fairly comprehensive, and that the findings are applicable to BMEOs throughout England and Wales.

The survey is, as far as we know, the most comprehensive and up-to-date survey of these organisations and provides, we believe, a fairly representative picture of black and minority ethnic organisations in England and, to a lesser extent, Wales. Care should be exercised, however, in extrapolating our data when it is based on subsections of questions where the response rate may be low.

Number and geographical distribution of BMEOs

We estimate[19] that there are currently more than 5000 BMEOs in England and Wales. This is based on our general assumptions about what constitutes an organisation, and takes into account the numbers of BMEOs in particular local authority areas, as compared with the minority ethnic population for these areas.

Many BMEOs operate in the inner city areas where the concentrations of ethnic

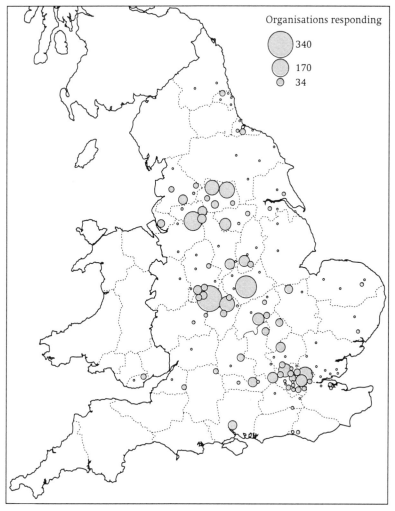

Figure 1 *Geographical distribution of BME voluntary organisations in database*

minority populations are highest, but significant numbers are located in the new towns and provincial centres, where a sizeable minority population can also be found.

The geographical area of operation of these organisations is an indicator of the extent to which they have a community base, as opposed to being more general

philanthropic organisations.

We asked those surveyed where their beneficiaries actually lived. Responses suggested that residents of the local neighbourhood, town or borough are by far the most likely beneficiaries. (See Figure 3 below.) This is particularly so in the case of organisations serving Bangladeshi people. Nearly two-thirds of

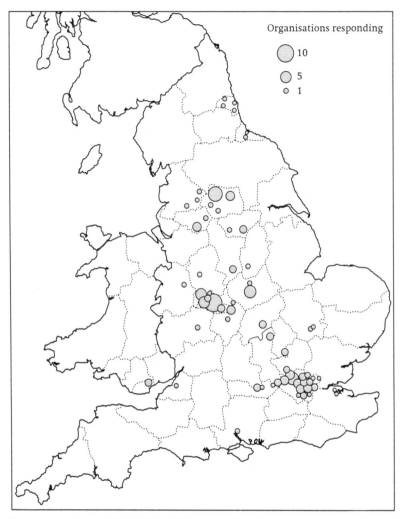

Figure 2 *Geographical distribution of organisations responding to the survey*

the BMEOs serving this community have a neighbourhood focus.

Organisations serving 'all black and ethnic minorities', Pakistani, or Caribbean clients are more likely to have a town or borough focus, while those serving the Chinese community tend to have a regional one. This is clearly connected with the settlement patterns of the various BME communities.[20] The Chinese community is generally found in small residential pockets spread over a wider region, while Bangladeshis tend to be more highly concentrated within relatively delimited residential areas. Organisations serving 'other BME' communities show an interesting pattern, in that they tend to be serving either a neighbourhood community or a regional community.

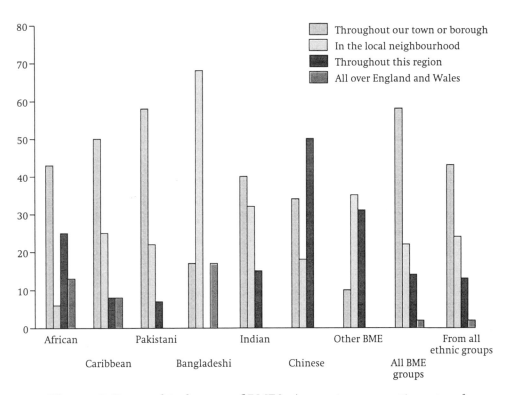

Figure 3 *Geographical range of BMEOs (percentage operating at each geographical scale)*

Our data confirm the observation made by many involved in the recent development of neighbourhood initiatives that most organisations serving minority ethnic groups have a wider-than-neighbourhood area of focus. Involving minority ethnic residents in a neighbourhood initiative is likely to require an engagement with community organisations with a wider-than-neighbourhood geographical remit, and more likely a borough/town one.

It is also apparent that a small number of BMEOs serve minority communities located in the rural areas or in relatively small towns. For example, Bedworth, a small town outside Coventry, has a West Indian Association comprising 16 members. Some Asian organisations also serve small minority ethnic communities in remote parts of the country.

There is little to suggest that BMEOs are particularly active in 'peripheral' housing estates, which is not surprising, given the low concentrations of ethnic minorities in such estates.[21] This has important implications for BMEO sustainability, given the tendency for government-sponsored regeneration initiatives to concentrate on these estates – sometimes to the exclusion of areas in which the ethnic minority population concentration is much higher.

The Single Regeneration Budget, Housing Action Trusts, Development Corporations and so on, have tended not to focus on areas with high BME concentrations. And some early New Deal for Communities areas also appeared to have the same deficiency. Recent guidance of some of these initiatives is, however, starting to shift the balance back. The fifth and sixth rounds of the Single Regeneration Budget and New Deal for Communities (and a lot of the Social Exclusion Unit's work on neighbourhood renewal) have long and strong passages stressing the importance of addressing the issues faced by BME communities.

Overall, our findings indicate that BMEOs emerge wherever there is a significant minority ethnic population. Data from Manchester and from some other parts of the country are not as comprehensive as we might have liked. However, we feel this is unlikely to alter the picture significantly.

We have concluded that the majority of BMEOs exist in the areas in which the minority ethnic population is greatest, regardless of local and regional conditions and policy environments. The lack of fully comprehensive data, however, throws up the question of whether local authorities, who are in a better position to get information about BMEOs in their area, should consider collecting this data in a more systematic way.

Governance

The way in which BMEOs are organised and run gives some indication of their role, relationship with the communities they serve and their likely sustainability.

The survey asked questions on legal status and governance as well as the length of time an organisation had been in existence. Out of the 200 respondents, 114 were charities, 43 companies limited by guarantee, 13 provident and friendly societies and 30 of no formal status.[22]

Charities included organisations such as: the Kokuma Dance Theatre Company; World Sikh Foundation; Nzambe Malangue Charity; Association of Jamaicans UK Trust; Organisation of Blind African Caribbeans; the Shree Vishwakara Association; and the Derby Asian Horticultural Centre. Many had a clear 'philanthropic' thrust, insofar as the beneficiaries of their efforts were not 'members' of the organisation.

Companies limited by guarantee included: PATH; Gateshead Visible Ethnic Minority Support Group; Independent Immigration Support Agency; Chinese Community School; and Birmingham Race Action Partnership. Many were either 'project based', on 'semi professional' lines, or local authority-supported ethnic minority forums.

Provident and friendly societies included: the Ad-dhuram Brotherhood; the Indian Workers Association; the African Women's Welfare Association; Arhag Housing Association; and

Huddersfield Harambee. As a whole, they were evenly divided between welfare and housing oriented organisations.

Non-formal associations were a mixed bag, which included arts and cultural organisations, young people's projects and Asian women's projects. Examples of 'other status' organisations included: the James Wiltshire Trust (help for blind people); Advancement of Prajapatis in Education; JCWI (anti-racism); Keighley Asian Business Forum; Multi-lingual Community Rights Group; LOCHMA (lovers of classical and contemporary music from home and abroad); and Asra Housing Association.

Judging from our survey (which may, admittedly, contain a higher proportion of more established organisations), 90 per cent of BMEOs have formal legal status, and, in the main, are autonomous, 'stand-alone' bodies. Most have duly constituted management committees, documented governance procedures, and hold regular, minuted, meetings. Almost two-thirds have been in existence for ten years or more. Thus, they are far from being a fleeting or ephemeral part of community life.

Most were started as self-help groups by people from a particular ethnic group and operate mainly on a local (neighbourhood or town/borough) basis. They could, therefore, be categorised as local self-help groups, were it not for two key features of their operations. Many are registered as charities, and are thus more formally established than the typical neighbourhood association. They

are also more likely to be serving people who are not members of the group – whether they live nearby, or in other parts of the town or region – and need, therefore, to be distinguished from residents' self-help groups.

This, together with the fact that only 10 per cent are established by the residents of a particular neighbourhood, suggests that BMEOs within the survey have a wider philanthropic function, closer to that of mainstream voluntary organisations than to relatively informal neighbourhood associations. Another way of putting this is to say that they operate from a local base but reach out beyond neighbourhood self help. This has a lot to do with the fact that minorities tend to be concentrated in a particular part of a town or city.

Furthermore, about a third of BMEOs have been established by individuals with a shared interest in a particular social issue or field of activity (rather than by residents of a particular neighbourhood). That is:

> ... three or four people in a front room saying 'Something must be done', about a health issue, educational under-performance, exclusions from school, racist attacks or harassment, care of the elderly, counselling, self-harm and suicide, cultural insensitivity of public bodies, discrimination in employment and services etc.[23]

Because of this, activities may cut across ethnic lines (for example, 'exclusion' is an issue facing all minority communities), and focus on specific sectors (such as education or health). This is why some BMEOs appear to operate on a fairly ad hoc, lobbying or campaigning basis which is not restricted to one particular geographical area.[24]

When, during the 1980s, local authorities and Training Enterprise Councils found themselves having to focus more and more on minority issues, it became essential that they deal with these special interest groups, who often had no legal status or public accountability procedures.

As the rules and regulations applying to the use of public funds were tightened, conditions for registering as a charity also became more stringent. The whole process could take two years or more. Establishing 'off-the-shelf' companies limited by guarantee, via the local authority legal department, became a fairly easy route to formalising local minority groups. This enabled them to become immediate recipients of public funding, avoiding the lengthy and time-consuming processes of registering as a charity.

This same era witnessed the emergence of black housing associations under the patronage of the Housing Corporation, being registered under the Provident and Friendly Act, and giving rise to yet another form of BMEO – the black housing association. The 'ring fencing' of Housing Corporation funds, aimed specifically at these organisations, is reflected in the fact that as our survey illustrates, they have become the largest, by far, of the BMEOs.

The seven housing associations which responded to the survey accounted for 66.5 per cent of the income (£36.5 million in 1998/99) of all respondent organisations, largely derived from trading income. Like many housing associations, they have grown over the last 20 years from relatively small organisations to much larger ones, with higher levels of resources. In particular, their activities have dramatically increased during the 1990s through the Housing Corporation's aim of increasing the share of housing provided by Registered Social Landlords to people from ethnic minorities.

There are however, still many small housing associations, such as those serving refugee communities and small minority ethnic groups, such as Somalis.

Very few BMEOs appear to have been established directly by mainstream agencies or already existing organisations, but those which have, such as Gateshead Visible Ethnic Minority Support Group and Birmingham Race Action Partnership are more likely to be serving beneficiaries from 'all BME groups'.

As for management, more than 75 per cent of the groups we surveyed have a management committee in which three-quarters or more of the members are from BME groups. This is particularly true of both provident and friendly societies, and those of non-formal status, who are also more likely to be serving one particular ethnic group. This suggests that the less formal 'ethnic associations' are focused particularly on helping specific ethnic groups, concentrated in one particular location. This tends to be confirmed by the fact that half of them are involved in no external networking at all – a much lower number than for other groups in this survey.

The organisations established by residents of a particular neighbourhood were most likely to be serving 'other BME' groups, which may indicate that they have been set up to meet the needs of a new immigrant or refugee population. Those established by 'a specific ethnic group', or as a 'self-help' group, are more likely to be serving African, Caribbean or Bangladeshi beneficiaries. (Chinese organisations are established by 'people with shared interests'.)

Charities and companies limited by guarantee are the types of organisation least likely to be serving a specific ethnic group, and more likely to be networking with other organisations. They also tend to have management committees with lower levels of black and minority ethnic representation.

Who do BMEOs serve?

The survey included questions on the characteristics of the main beneficiaries of the organisations, including ethnic origin, demographic characteristics and category of need (for example ex-offenders, refugees, people with disabilities and those who are unemployed). More than one of the demographic characteristics and categories of need could be selected by respondents.

In the 1999 Home Office LOVAS study of Smethwick, only 5 per cent of mainstream voluntary organisations' beneficiaries were from a particular ethnic or minority group, whereas 10 per cent of community organisations' beneficiaries were. In contrast, 53 per cent of organisations we surveyed focused specifically on beneficiaries from mainly one ethnic group, and a further 23 per cent focused on all black and minority ethnic groups. A quarter served people from all ethnic groups, including white.

Compared with the mainstream voluntary and community sectors, BMEOs are clearly most closely focused on ethnic minority beneficiaries.

As far as the individual demographic characteristics of main beneficiaries are concerned:

- more than 70 per cent of the organisations served adult women;
- 63 per cent served adult men;
- 58 per cent served young people aged 16 to 25 years;
- 54 per cent served the elderly; and
- 41 per cent served school-age children.

Three-quarters of the charities were serving adult women and, to a lesser extent, older men, as also were companies limited by guarantee. Provident and friendly societies focused more on young and elderly people, or on whole families – which fits with the fact that many of them are housing related. Non-formal BMEOs cater particularly to the needs of young people and women, and 'other

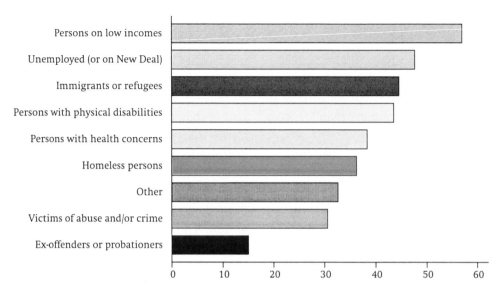

Figure 4 *Characteristics of BMEO beneficiaries (percentage of BMEOs serving each type of beneficiary)*

status' BMEOs to adults, both male and female.

In terms of category of need, charities serve a fairly broad spread of beneficiaries. Companies limited by guarantee are more likely to be dealing with clients on low incomes or unemployed, while two-thirds of the provident and friendly societies serve homeless people on low incomes.

Non-formal BMEOs are also concerned with people on low incomes, but they are particularly associated with 'other' types of beneficiary. Over half of the 'other status' BMEOs are focused on physical disabilities (a figure surpassed only by provident and friendly societies) or on unemployed or low income groups (see Tables 2 and 3 below).

It is worth noting (given the common stereotype that black people, particularly young African Caribbean

men, are perpetrators of crime), that twice as many of the organisations we surveyed were dealing with victims of abuse or crime than were dealing with ex-offenders and probationers.

In summary, BMEOs are established mainly, but not exclusively, to serve particular ethnic communities, sometimes on a neighbourhood basis, but sometimes on a town-wide or even regional basis, reflecting the particular residential pattern of the community concerned. They tend to serve persons on low incomes, or who are unemployed, or who have health problems or disabilities. Refugees or newly arrived immigrants are also particularly likely to be beneficiaries.

Few organisations are established exclusively by residents of a particular neighbourhood. This tends to imply that although sometimes established on the

Table 2 *Beneficiaries and interest groups served by legal status of organisation (percentages by legal status)*

	Registered charity	Company limited by guarantee	Provident or friendly society	No formal legal status/ other status	All	Per cent of all organis- ations
Beneficiaries						
Pre-school children	28.7	31.6	30.8	12.5	43.0	24.0
School age children	43.5	36.8	38.5	39.6	73.0	40.8
Young people (16–24)	58.3	63.2	53.8	56.3	103.0	57.5
Adults – men	63.0	65.8	53.8	62.5	112.0	62.6
Adults – women	76.9	78.9	46.2	64.6	126.0	70.4
Elderly people	58.3	50.0	53.8	47.9	97.0	54.2
Single parents	48.1	52.6	46.2	37.5	79.0	44.1
Whole families	53.7	60.5	53.8	39.6	89.0	49.7
All beneficiaries	**100.0**	**100.0**	**100.0**	**100.0**	**100.0**	**100.0**
Interest groups						
Ex-offenders or probationers	16.2	16.2	25.0	12.2	24.0	14.8
Immigrants or refugees	45.5	43.2	33.3	43.9	70.0	43.2
Victims of abuse and/or crime	33.3	32.4	33.3	29.3	48.0	29.6
Persons on low incomes	54.5	67.6	66.7	51.2	90.0	55.6
Homeless persons	40.4	35.1	58.3	24.4	57.0	35.2
Persons with physical disabilities	40.4	37.8	58.3	46.3	68.0	42.0
Persons with health concerns	41.4	32.4	25.0	36.6	60.0	37.0
Unemployed (or on New Deal)	49.5	62.2	50.0	36.6	75.0	46.3
Other	20.2	24.3	41.7	48.8	51.0	31.5
All interest groups	**100.0**	**100.0**	**100.0**	**100.0**	**100.0**	**100.0**

Table 3 *Beneficiaries and interest groups served by main ethnic groups (percentages by ethnic group)*

	African Caribbean	Pakistani	Bangladeshi	Indian	Chinese	Other BME	From all BME groups	From all ethnic groups
Beneficiaries								
Pre-school children	40.0	16.7	28.6	0.0	24.0	42.9	15.0	25.0	20.9
School-age children	46.7	16.7	21.4	33.3	48.0	42.9	40.0	47.5	46.5
Young people (16–24)	80.0	50.0	50.0	33.3	48.0	42.9	45.0	67.5	62.8
Adults – men	86.7	66.7	57.1	50.0	76.0	57.1	60.0	62.5	53.5
Adults – women	80.0	6.7	64.3	66.7	76.0	57.1	65.0	82.5	62.8
Elderly people	53.3	83.3	42.9	33.3	68.0	42.9	60.0	42.5	55.8
Single parents	60.0	41.7	35.7	16.7	52.0	28.6	40.0	45.0	48.5
Whole families	46.7	33.3	42.9	16.7	60.0	57.1	60.0	47.5	53.5
All	**100.0**	**100.0**	**100.0**	**100.0**	**100.0**	**100.0**	**100.0**	**100.0**	**100.0**
Interest groups								
Ex-offenders or probationers	42.9	20.0	0.0	0.0	14.3	0.0	11.8	13.2	17.5
Immigrants or refugees	64.3	20.0	33.3	16.7	28.6	33.3	70.6	44.7	47.5
Victims of abuse and/ or crime	35.7	10.0	25.0	33.3	33.3	0.0	23.5	34.2	35.0
Persons on low incomes	78.6	50.0	50.0	33.3	57.1	16.7	35.3	71.1	55.0
Homeless persons	50.0	40.0	8.3	16.7	33.3	0.0	29.4	31.6	50.0

Table 3 *continued*

	African Caribbean		Pakistani Bangladeshi		Indian Chinese		Other BME	From all BME groups	From all ethnic groups
Persons with physical disabilities	50.0	40.0	50.0	16.7	47.6	0.0	35.3	44.7	45.0
Persons with health concerns	78.6	40.0	25.0	16.7	47.6	33.3	5.9	36.8	40.0
Unemployed (or on New Deal)	64.3	40.0	41.7	33.3	47.6	16.7	35.3	55.3	47.5
Other	28.6	30.0	41.7	33.3	47.6	50.0	17.6	21.1	32.5
All	100.0	100.0	100.0	100.0	100.0	100.0	100.0	100.0	100.0

basis of self-help or by a particular ethnic group, BMEOs emerge from already existing ethnic linkages, often covering a wider geographical area. They arise from within the network of cultural, religious, economic and kinship ties that bind together BME communities.

Services provided

In the LOVAS study of Smethwick, the most common type of voluntary organisation was found to be general voluntary service organisations, followed by youth groups, then health and disability services.

The most frequently reported activities carried out by the voluntary groups were recreation, advice and education (19 per cent) and non-expert help and support (12.4 per cent). More than a third of them did not deal at all with social problems or issues. In the community sector, sports and leisure associations, religious-based community self-help (13 per cent) and trade associations (7 per cent) were the most common types, while recreation (47 per cent), advice and education (13 per cent) and 'opportunities for association' were the most frequently mentioned activities. Over half of these groups reported that they did not deal with social issues.

Our survey also asked organisations about their main field of activity and the services they provided to beneficiaries. The main service provided by BMEOs is 'advocacy and advice', such as legal and immigration advice and equal opportunities and anti-racism advocacy (17 per cent). The next most commonly provided services are in the area of health, including mental health (14 per cent) and welfare and income support (just over 11 per cent). Dealing with social issues is clearly very much part of their work.

Housing and accommodation, and (school related) education – the fourth and fifth most commonly mentioned activities (11 per cent each) – highlight the concern for 'community' welfare, particularly as mainstream service provision in these communities is often sadly lacking.

It is noticeable that few BMEOs appear to concentrate exclusively on one particular service. The majority are involved in at least two or three, and some straddle a much wider range. There is a degree of specialisation, but many could, with justice, be described as 'general welfare providers'.

This general welfare function applies to organisations whatever ethnic group they serve. Different ethnic groups are provided with access to pretty much the same range of BMEO services (or, in some cases, such as environmental improvement, the lack of services).

There is a slight bias, however, towards BMEOs serving particular ethnic communities specialising in particular types of activity. Organisations serving the African and Caribbean communities, for example, are slightly more inclined to be involved in health-related services, while those serving the Pakistani community are more likely to spend time on general advice and advocacy.

In the case of the African Caribbean community, the most likely explanation for the focus on health is the significant levels of involvement of West Indian women in nursing. Health issues, such as AIDS, sickle cell, or glaucoma, may also play a part.

As for the Pakistani community, many people, particularly elders, are not comfortable with the English language. 'Go-betweens' (representatives) at the local community centre (or mosque, etc) who can act as advisors and advocates are often the best way to negotiate access into the state welfare system.

With respect to legal status, charities generally cover a whole range of activities, but are particularly likely to be involved in health or welfare. This may well be because local and health authorities, who are responsible for providing care services, are the main source of funding for these charities.

Companies limited by guarantee are more involved in advice and training, while provident and friendlies show a clear bias towards housing (more than 30 per cent), and non-formal organisations towards education, arts and sports.

In summary, the survey paints an overall picture of BMEOs as providers of a wide range of educational, advisory, and welfare services for particular ethnic communities (although a number do serve all ethnic groups). Some of the larger ones are specialist providers of particular types of service (such as the black housing associations or the Sickle Cell Association), and some of the smaller ones focus exclusively on cultural and leisure activities. But the majority provide a full range of 'welfare oriented' services (including advocacy) to

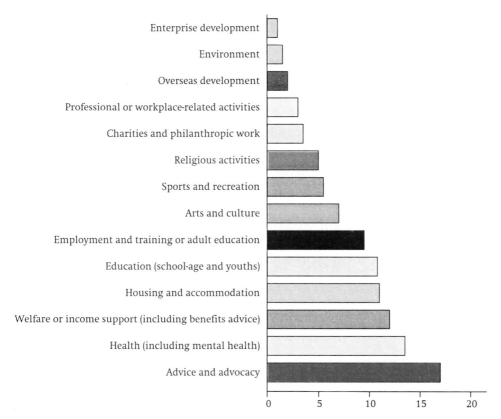

Figure 5 *Percentage of BMEO time spent on particular service activities*

the more disadvantaged members of the 'community' at large.

There are four main elements to these 'welfare oriented' services:

1. providing a focus for social networking both inside and outside the community;
2. providing culturally oriented services, aimed at preserving group cohesion and identity;
3. providing support and welfare services on a pastoral basis; and
4. providing advisory advocacy services which help community members to access mainstream provision.

In the latter capacity, BMEOs act as mediators between the local minority communities and the wider welfare state.

Three sustainability issues stand out with respect to the type of services provided:

1. Will black and minority ethnic communities continue to use BMEOs as a way of preserving cultural identity and of maintaining social ties? (We discuss this at the end of this chapter.)
2. Do mainstream service agencies recognise BMEOs as being of impor-

tance in providing service to the BME communities? And if they do, will they provide them with the necessary resources? (We take up this question in Chapter 4.)

3. Will BMEOs continue to be seen as a means of gaining access to mainstream services? Or will the move to more formal status, funded by mainstream bodies, force them to become primarily direct deliverers of services, among other 'mainstream' deliverers?

Public perception - interviews with local residents

As part of our case studies, some 300 black and minority ethnic residents of Birmingham and Brent, both areas of high minority ethnic concentration, were interviewed to establish their views on the role of minority ethnic-led organisations in providing services to the community. We felt the postal survey of the voluntary sector organisations gave only a partial picture of the issues. The sustainability of BMEOs is clearly contingent in large part upon support from the community.

Birmingham (Soho/Handsworth) and Brent were chosen because they were in major conurbations with a large number of black and minority ethnic residents and because each had a mix of the various minority ethnic communities. Using estimates of the population based on census data, we calculated target numbers of 'young' (16 to 29), 'adult' (30 to 49) and 'older' (aged over 50) people to interview.

In Handsworth, Birmingham, 140 people were interviewed during the latter part of 1999. Respondents were selected at random, either on the street in various parts of Soho and Handsworth, or in mixed tenure households in the same area. They represented approximately 1 per cent of the minority ethnic population of the area. A list of some 80 BMEOs thought to be operating in the area was compiled in advance, and this was used as a prompt in order to remind respondents, where necessary, of the names of organisations providing particular types of service.

A similar exercise was carried out in the adjoining areas of Stonebridge and Alperton in the London Borough of Brent. The first is a very poor area with a high concentration of African Caribbean people. The second is more prosperous, and has a high proportion of Asian residents.

Respondents were asked the same types of questions in different ways, so that recognition of particular organisations was not hindered by unfamiliarity. They were asked, for example, about voluntary organisations, community groups, centres, clubs, associations and charities,[25] so that there was no misunderstanding based upon particular notions of voluntary or community organisations.

The most striking finding of all was the low awareness of BMEOs shown by most of the individuals surveyed. The large majority of respondents had little awareness of black or minority-led voluntary groups (or clubs or associations), or of the services they provide. Many were not able even to give a specific example of one. It must be acknowledged, though that similar responses would probably have come from white individuals asked about white voluntary organisations.[26]

The percentage of people interviewed who could mention voluntary groups that they knew were run by minority ethnic groups was only 33 per cent in Alperton, 25 per cent in Handsworth, and 8 per cent in Stonebridge. Although about twice as many people mentioned voluntary organisations which they believed were minority-run, these included organisations such as sports centres and libraries, which were incorrectly identified as BMEOs.

Of the respondents who knew of BMEOs, most had either used them, or worked for them. They were also asked for their views on these organisations.

Although the following views were expressed by only a handful of people surveyed, they were worrying:

they are seen as incompetent and badly managed... this has to change.

they need to promote themselves more... I don't really know what they do, or how well they do it.

they need... a professional approach... more accountable to the community.

they haven't got the facilities of white organisations.

they need to improve their image.

they need to move into proper offices and act more professional.

You must be joking – I wouldn't give them a penny – What!! to party with – Cheow!! – You's a black man – would you?

scruffy surroundings.

Other views were more sympathetic:

it's not their fault – they are under-resourced.

it's about time a [mental health] project was set up by our own people.

[BMEOs] show them [the local authority] we can do things for ourselves... not puppets.

no one else is interested in black kids. No one cares [about ethnic minority children being excluded from schools].

it's [Saturday school] changed the whole attitude to education around here.

teaches us the importance of our culture and religion.

[I now know] what to do about sickle cell.

if we're not provided with services, we've got to do it for ourselves.

only [the] association [can do it] – whites don't cater for ethnic weddings.

[give]... good advice about benefits and housing grant.

One even acknowledged the dilemma the BMEOs were in, always having to prove themselves on shoestring budgets and resources:

> black mismanagement – white people love to hear that.

This finding raises some anxieties – although white people may have similar views about how white voluntary organisations could be better run (there are no comparative data). The danger is that any criticism of BMEOs could – perhaps wrongly – confirm the popular stereotype that money is being thrown away on useless inner-city projects. If there are valid concerns about the way these organisations are run, then we would argue that this is a matter for the funders of these organisations, such as local authorities, to investigate, and to ensure that 'capacity building' funds (see Chapter 3) are being channelled in the right directions.

In other ways, the finding is perhaps unsurprising. There is widespread recognition of the fact that participation in voluntary sector activities in Britain has been declining for some time. This may affect the black and minority ethnic communities' awareness of BMEOs disproportionately as, given it is such a small sector to start with, the involvement of fewer black people is likely to make the presence of BMEOs even less obvious.

Certainly the level of involvement in voluntary activities was low by those questioned. Many respondents mentioned that they had no time to be involved in them, even if they wanted to be. Others, apparently surprised to hear of BMEOs operating in their geographical area, suggested that they should 'advertise themselves more'. Similarly, respondents who did know of BMEOs sometimes expressed the opinion that they should 'move away from the back streets' and locate themselves where they were more easily accessible to the greatest number of people.

The finding also needs to be interpreted in the light of the low level of volunteering traditionally associated with the BME communities. The Volunteer Centre UK, for example, found that volunteers, in general, are most likely to be middle-aged and to come from the higher socio-economic groups. 'Black people are under-represented as volunteers'.[27] (However, see the discussion in Chapter 3.)

A number of younger respondents stated that they had used a particular BMEO during their early years, but did so no longer. A young Asian respondent, for example, had, as a schoolboy, attended sports training sessions at a black-led neighbourhood organisation. Now, however, he attended a local further education college, where sporting facilities far surpassed those offered by the BMEO. As a result, he was no longer in contact with the latter. Young people in particular, especially students, may find that the services which most interest them are more readily available through mainstream bodies.

Notwithstanding the above, respondents did, on the whole, show a higher awareness of general services available within the community as a whole, including social security offices, sports and social clubs, colleges, nurseries and post offices. These were often given as examples of community organisations known to the respondent.

Handsworth Leisure Centre, for example, which is operated by the city council, was the most frequently mentioned organisation by all respondents in Birmingham. Some actually put it forward as an example of a black-led organisation. This, perhaps, reflects that many of this centre's staff are of minority ethnic origin. Many residents were not concerned to distinguish between community services delivered by minorities, and those actually run by minorities.

Similarly, in Stonebridge, residents of a housing estate that is being 'regenerated' gave the names of organisations which had been set up by the local Housing Action Trust – again with black staff.

These examples highlight the fact that members of the BME communities may be more interested in whether a particular service is provided (and how it is provided) than whether it is run by a BMEO as such. This must be weighed against the fact that some respondents indicated specifically that 'black' or 'Asian' organisations should be given every opportunity to provide services to black and minority ethnic communities.

It is also important to note that religious bodies, or organisations closely associated with them, were clearly connected in the minds of many respondents with the types of services we were asking about. Activities connected with 'my church group' or 'the temple' (or mosque), were routinely put forward as examples, without prompting, along with the question 'Is that the type of thing you mean?'

Certain organisations were frequently mentioned – the Asian Resource Centre in Handsworth and the Brent Indian Association in Alperton, for example. Both of these organisations have a strong high street presence and act as information and advice centres, as well as providing individual client counselling. Both organisations were visited by the researchers and both evidenced a large number of users.

In Stonebridge, which is predominantly an African Caribbean area, the Bridge Park Centre was the most frequently mentioned BMEO by residents, although many appeared not to use it. The centre, in fact, has achieved a degree of notoriety as an African Caribbean 'flagship' project which was closed down. A similar fate beset another flagship African Caribbean organisation, the Handsworth Employment Scheme (HES) in Birmingham. Although it is not appropriate to analyse the reason for these closures here, they do underline the importance of the issue of sustainability for high profile, resource-intensive black-led voluntary projects.

In both Stonebridge and Handsworth, some African Caribbean respondents pointed to the fact that organisations that had once been vibrant and active, and had demonstrated clearly that they were meeting local demand, were now no longer in existence. This was most commonly attributed to a lack of funding for African Caribbean projects caused perhaps, as one respondent put it, by not 'having enough black councillors', or, as others would have it, purely through 'racism' and 'neglect'.

This underscores a feeling that was frequently expressed by African Caribbean respondents that many 'black' organisations had been closed down as a result of funding cuts. Some respondents in Handsworth even contrasted this with the apparently thriving state of Asian organisations in the area (pointing, for example, to a newly built temple along the Soho Road).

The evidence from our study does not overall support the conclusion that BMEOs serving one particular ethnic group are any more likely to be successful than those serving others. However, the responses do underline the possibility that awareness of BMEOs may not be high in certain communities simply because many of the more prominent organisations have been shut down.

For users of local BMEOs, whether Asian or African Caribbean, the main benefits obtained from the organisations were, in order of the frequency of mention:

- general advice and information;
- specific guidance (in areas such as employment);

- opportunities for the pursuit of cultural interests; and
- day care facilities for elderly people.

Householders were asked whether anyone in the house had difficulties in the areas of health, education, language or physical disability. They were also asked if the household contained any elderly people, or school and pre-school age children, and, if so, whether BMEOs helped to meet any of their needs. The benefits from using BMEOs at the household level were (again ranked in frequency of mention order):

- specific guidance;
- general guidance;
- access to services provided by another agency; and
- opportunities for meeting cultural needs.

In the case of the first three benefits, BMEOs appear to act as an interface between the household and mainstream bodies providing services geared to particular needs. Even the fourth can, to some extent, be seen in this light. Opportunities for learning or improving English were commonly mentioned by Asian respondents, particularly in Alperton.

A small number of respondents mentioned the needs of pre-school children, particularly in connection with nurseries, some of which were BMEOs. In the case of school-age children, after-school activities were quite often mentioned (but not specifically BMEO-related). Day care facilities were often mentioned for elderly people.

The survey of residents in Brent threw up another interesting finding. A number of respondents mentioned Age Concern, and similar agencies with a 'high street presence'.

On following this up we found that the manager of the local Age Concern shop considered his organisation to be a BMEO. Age Concern in fact operates on a federated basis, the national organisation providing support for independent local bodies. Other charities mentioned, such as Red Cross, may operate in a similar manner. There are, therefore, interesting questions about relationships at the local level between mainstream bodies and affiliated BMEOs which are not otherwise mentioned in this report.

Change in the community

Minority ethnic groups are themselves in transition, some groups are further on with creating an identity that is able to retain the distinctiveness of their respective cultures whilst also adapting to become an integral part of British society.[28]

Minority ethnic communities are themselves subject to change. The age structure of the population; second and third generation attitudes towards traditional cultures; family and gender relation patterns; the employment aspirations of different community members etc, all point to BME communities of tomorrow that in at least some

ways, will be different from the BME communities of today.

One of the great advantages of speaking to people in the community was that it gave us a chance to find out about people's perceptions of how the community was changing – and how this might impact on the type of services that the community would require in future.

The minority ethnic population in Britain is gradually ageing, but there is also a rapidly growing number of young people from black and minority ethnic groups. Individuals interviewed overwhelmingly expressed a desire for something to be done for older and for young people. For elderly people, the need 'for some sort of convenient spot where the elderly could meet with others and socialise' was voiced. For young people, the need for affordable leisure facilities was frequently mentioned. There was a clear sense that BMEOs had a role to play in helping youngsters to access leisure facilities, but less certainty as to whether they could actually succeed in this.

A young African Caribbean male in Handsworth suggested, for example that escalating, drug-related, black-on-black violence was creating an untenable environment. BMEOs had proven themselves powerless to stop this, 'despite all these government announcements about giving money to black people'. In the 'dog-eat-dog' situation in which he and his friends lived, 'you've got to be your own voluntary organisation'.

Some of the people we interviewed actually worked or were volunteers for BMEOs. They frequently raised issues around the image of BMEOs, which are often portrayed as being inefficient or incompetent. If they were to play a role in the future delivery of services, they would need to 'project a more "professional" image' and 'advertise their services more widely'.

Some respondents saw the age of many of the BMEO leaders who were heading up the traditional associations as a potential problem. They were 'too set in their ways' or were 'hanging on to traditions which no longer interest the young people'. Others, however, thought that this was all part of the normal relationship between generations, and that the young would eventually take up the mantle of their elders and continue to maintain the customs and traditions of the group.

During our fieldwork in Alperton, we had a long discussion with the secretary of the Hindu Association, who indicated that this was a live topic of debate in Hindu Associations up and down the country.

A closely related issue came up when respondents were asked whether black- and/or Asian-led organisations ought to be providing more services for the community. Asian respondents, in particular, tended to be roughly divided on the issue. Some suggested that this only encouraged an inward-looking insularity which 'will never get us anywhere'. Others assumed that services should be 'delivered by people who actually sympathise with our needs, and don't turn their eyes away when they're standing right in front of us'.

Many of the changes that are taking place within Britain's minority ethnic communities go beyond the scope of this study. However, it is clear that these changes will make some impact on the future development of BMEOs. The direction taken by youth groups, or women's groups, for example, will be of importance. Sporting and cultural associations may well start to appear more appealing than welfare clubs, or the more traditional Hindu or West Indian association. BMEOs themselves may become irrelevant to those who have access to university and college, and, through them, to other mainstream facilities.

It would obviously be hazardous to try to predict, on the basis of our limited research, how these changes will affect BMEOs, but several scenarios seem possible:

1. BMEOs recognise the need to change with changing times and take effective steps to win over younger recruits;
2. younger people maintain their interest in cultural identity and accept that BMEOs are a necessary part of this (while perhaps working for reform);
3. BMEOs concentrate on serving the needs of an increasingly elderly beneficiary population in the traditional way;

4. newer, up-and-coming BMEOs replace some of the existing ones; and
5. BMEOs become irrelevant to all but the most disadvantaged members of the community.

Only further, more detailed research could help establish which of these scenarios is most likely, but the evidence from our own work suggests that some BMEOs are well aware of the issues and are taking steps to ensure their own survival.

Minority groups have developed forms of coping with the change that is occurring, including reliance on community spirit and spirituality, a sharing of history and developing strong ethnic group role models. This is aimed particularly at the younger generation.[29]

3. The Resource Base

We wanted to obtain a picture of resource base and resource flows to black and minority ethnic organisations in order to assess their sustainability.

The common perception of BMEOs is that they tend to suffer continual funding crises and have a poor funding base. But this picture was not entirely borne out by our research. However, the picture may, in part, be distorted by the number of large organisations, such as housing associations, which responded to our postal questionnaire. There is the possibility that the smallest organisations were not in as good a position to respond.

In order to get a clearer idea of what was going on, we grouped our respondents according to their financial income raised during 1998/99. 'Small' organisations received up to £50,000; 'medium'-sized organisations from £50,000 to £250,000; and 'large' organisations more than £250,000.

The postal survey asked a number of questions in relation to these issues, which were also the subject of discussions undertaken with local organisations as part of the case studies carried out in Birmingham and Brent. (See Appendix I for a list of the organisations contacted.)

Funding

The voluntary organisations in the survey were classified into three size bands on the basis of their income during the financial year 1998/99.

The pie charts in Figure 6 reveal huge differences in the nature of funding of the three types of organisation.

Small organisations (up to £50,000) received about half their funding from local authority grants. The two other most important sources of income are members' contributions and charities, each of which contributes around a sixth of their income.

Medium-sized organisations (£50,000 to £250,000) have more diverse sources of funding. The largest single source is still local authority grants, accounting for just under a third of their income. The National Lottery and contracts with statutory bodies are the other largest sources of income. Together, these account for three-fifths of their income. The largest part of the rest of their income is provided by charities and other statutory bodies.

Large organisations (those with incomes of more than £250,000 – which include most of the housing associations which responded to the survey) raised the great bulk of their funding (77 per cent) from trading activities.

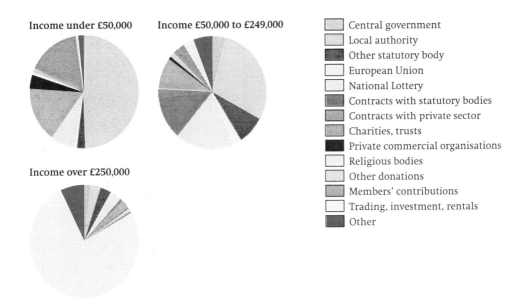

Income under £50,000   Income £50,000 to £249,000

☐ Central government
☐ Local authority
■ Other statutory body
☐ European Union
☐ National Lottery
▨ Contracts with statutory bodies
▨ Contracts with private sector
▨ Charities, trusts
■ Private commercial organisations
☐ Religious bodies
☐ Other donations
▨ Members' contributions
☐ Trading, investment, rentals
■ Other

Income over £250,000

Figure 6 *Contrasts in funding sources (slices represent percentage of income from each source)*

The large organisations received nearly four-fifths of the income of all BMEOs responding to the survey (Table 4). They received nearly all the trading income, and two-thirds of the funding from central government and other statutory bodies.

However, medium-sized organisations received three-quarters of the income derived from contracts with statutory bodies, and over three-fifths of income from local authorities and the National Lottery. Charity funding was equally split between medium-sized and large organisations, while funding from religious bodies went to medium-sized and small organisations.

Funding and status

Differences in the sources of funding,

depending on the size of the group, gave an important indication of the stability of the sector as a whole.

The smallest organisations, being mainly dependent upon grant income, are the most vulnerable to cycles in funding and the short-term and discontinuous nature of grant funding. With much of their remaining income made up from members' contributions, their financial position is the weakest.

In contrast, large organisations are much more financially sustainable, having built up an income stream from their commercial operations. The largest are housing associations, which also receive (in England) government funding via the Housing Corporation.

Medium-sized organisations are the most dependent upon providing subcontracted services. They are, therefore,

Table 4 Distribution of funds by size of organisation and funding source

	Income				Per cent of organisation's income				Per cent of all funding received from each source		
	Up to £50k	£50–£249k	Over £250k	All BMEOs	Up to £50k	£50–£249k	Over £250k	All BMEOs	Up to £50k	£50–£249k	Over £250k
Central government	5631	273,461	614,593	893,685	1.0	4.2	2.2	2.5	0.6	30.6	68.8
Lcoal authority	272,285	1,898,233	821,159	2,991,677	48.8	28.9	2.9	8.5	9.1	63.5	27.4
Otehr statutory body	13,708	539,507	920,382	1,473,597	2.5	8.2	3.3	4.2	0.9	36.6	62.5
European Union	4250	171,340	252,822	428,412	0.8	2.6	0.9	1.2	1.0	40.0	59.0
National Lottery	40,333	1,124,072	671,693	1,836,098	7.2	17.1	2.4	5.2	2.2	61.2	36.6
Contracts with statutory bodies	0	808,427	300,213	1,108,640	2.0	12.3	1.1	3.1	0.0	72.9	27.1
Contracts with private sector	0	170,015	25,000	195,015	0.0	2.6	0.1	0.6	0.0	87.2	12.8
Charities, trusts	89,639	599,759	662,778	1,352,177	16.1	9.1	2.3	3.8	6.6	44.4	49.0
Private commercial organisations	22,360	50,992	27,500	100,852	4.0	0.8	0.1	0.3	22.2	50.6	27.3
Religious bodies	3148	4202	0	7350	0.6	0.1	0.0	0.0	42.8	57.2	0.0
Other donations	7694	95,451	272,509	375,653	1.4	1.5	1.0	1.1	2.0	25.4	72.5
Members' contributions	86,996	245,858	155,518	488,373	15.6	3.7	0.6	1.4	17.8	50.3	31.8
Trading, investment, rentals	3664	200,869	21,537,041	21,741,574	0.7	3.1	76.2	61.4	0.0	0.9	99.1
Other	9676	388,308	2,011,908	2,408,892	1.6	5.9	7.1	6.8	0.4	16.1	83.5
Sum of all sources	558,383	6,570,495	28,273,117	35,401,995	100.0	100.0	100.0	100.0	1.6	18.6	79.9
Total income of organisation	724,445	6,975,255	28,784,811	36,484,511	100.0	100.0	100.0				

vulnerable to the changing financial position and policies of the organisations they subcontract to, but in a stronger overall position than the smallest organisations.

Legal status

Smaller organisations are the most likely to have no formal legal status. Larger organisations are mainly companies limited by guarantee (for the reasons outlined in Chapter 2) and registered charities. However, nearly a fifth of the largest are also provident or friendly societies.

Number of employees and volunteers

BMEOs without a legal status tend to be small in terms of income. Fewer than half (18) had any employees. Those BMEOs with formal status were more likely to employ between four and seven people. Overall, the mean number of people that non-formal BMEOs employed was less than half that of formally constituted organisations. Unsurprisingly, BMEOs with the largest incomes tended to have the largest numbers of employees.

However, BMEOs without a formal status had a slightly larger number of volunteers on average than those with a formal status. BMEOs with incomes from £50,000 to £250,000 had the largest average number of volunteers. These organisations also had the highest average number of volunteer hours per

organisation – nearly three times that for small or informal BMEOs. One slightly surprising finding was that the mean number of hours worked per volunteer was smallest in the BMEOs with the lowest incomes and without a formal legal status.

Origins and size

There is not a great deal of difference in the origins of these organisations by size. Most BMEOs of all sizes were established by particular minority communities, though the smaller organisations and those with no formal status were most likely to have started as self-help groups or to have been set up by individuals with shared interests.

Overview

The main source of income (more than three-fifths of the total) for all BMEOs in the last financial year was income from trading. But this average is distorted by the incomes of the largest BMEOS, in particular the housing associations, which derive relatively high levels of income from their trading activities (and account for more than 99 per cent of trading income for all BMEOs). Other key sources of funds included local authorities, central government, the National Lottery Charities Board, statutory bodies and charities.

For the most common type of organisation in our survey (income of £50,000 to £250,000), local authority funding was the most significant source of

Table 5 *Legal status by size of organisation (percentage of all in income band)*

Status	Up to £50k	£50– £249k	Over £250k
Registered charity	46.9	84.1	68.8
Trust	3.1	0.0	0.0
Company limited by guarantee	4.7	36.5	56.3
Provident or friendly society	9.4	1.6	18.8
No formal legal status	23.4	1.6	6.3
Other status	20.3	4.8	0.0
Number (100%)	64	63	16

support, with a total of £1.9 million coming from that source, followed by the National Lottery Charities Board (£1.1 million).

The operating costs of most BMEOs are roughly in line with their income – only a small number generate a significant surplus or accumulate large losses.

Income over the past five years had been rising for almost half the organisations, pretty much regardless of organisational size. (Only 37 per cent of organisations in the LOVAS survey of Smethwick had experienced a similar rise, and this was mainly restricted to the larger organisations.) Similarly, more than 40 per cent expected income to grow in 1999/2000, and less than 20 per cent expected a decline.

The main sources of income for 'informal' BMEOs were grants from the local authority and members' contributions, followed by grants from the National Lottery and funding from charities. These organisations accounted for nearly a fifth of all funding from members' contributions going to BMEOs.

The ethnic background of beneficiaries bears no significant relationship to past levels of income, or to expectations about future growth. It is of some significance to note, however, that organisations serving 'other BME' groups – which include refugees and asylum seekers – appeared to be particularly optimistic about future income.

As mentioned elsewhere in this report, these organisations are more likely to have been established by 'residents of a particular area' – probably the very areas in which newly arrived asylum seekers have been settled, and where there is already an established ethnic minority community. Given the high profile the issue of asylum seekers has had in recent years, it is probable that organisations assisting in their settlement (in the areas of housing, employment, advice etc) expect more government funding to be available for this purpose.

Overall, the findings provide convincing evidence that BMEOs are sustainable from a financial point of view – assum-

Table 6 *Employment by size and status of organisation (percentage of all in size band)*

Number of employees	Number of BMEOs	Income band			Legal status	
		Up to £50k	£50–£249k	Over £250k	Formal	Informal
1–3	22	29.2	20.6	13.3	24.8	11.1
4–7	47	54.2	46.0	33.3	43.1	83.3
8 or more	33	16.7	33.3	53.3	32.1	5.6
Number with employees	102	24	63	15	109	18

ing that there are no major cutbacks in the main sources of income. This is not to imply that they are particularly well resourced, but that the majority (though by no means all) appear to be getting by, even though they are not generating reserves. Our discussion with the National Lotteries Charity Board suggests that there is unlikely to be a cutback in funding to BMEOs from this source, at least in the short term.

What is of more concern is that in addition to the possibility of further local authority cutbacks, the new statutory funding regimes which are currently being introduced may not provide the same levels of financial support to BMEOs as there have been in the past.

This could affect all BMEOs, but less so the housing associations (who are mainly funded through the Housing Corporation) and those which are currently more self-reliant through membership contributions. In general,

the groups able to lever resources from health zones, education zones, new deal and SRB partnerships are less likely to be affected. But it is not clear at the moment which ones will be able to do this. This issue is taken up in the next chapter.

Facilities and premises

In order to assess further the sustainability of BMEOs, we asked them about the types of facility they provide, and about their access to premises and equipment.

It may be felt that this is a rather limited indication of an organisation's sustainability (it could end up owning a property in a poor area of a city or be saddled with a property which was a liability). However, ownership and equity issues are at the heart of racial inequalities and, more generally, poverty and disadvantage. For many organisations, the need for independence also seemed to be quite important.

Table 7 *Employees and volunteers, by size of organisation*

Variable	Measure	Income band			Legal status	
		Up to £50k	£50–£249k	Over £250k	Formal	Informal
Number of employees	Mean number per BMEO	1.9	6.2	7.4	4.8	2.0
	Total across all BMEOs	128	391	119	671	96
	BMEOs returning data	66	63	16	139	48
Number of volunteers	Mean number per BMEO	7.4	12.5	10.4	9.6	10.2
	Total across all BMEOs	287	500	83	822	234
	BMEOs returning data	39	40	8	86	23
Volunteer hours	Mean number per BMEO	29.0	87.7	72.3	65.9	34.6
	Total across all BMEOs	958	3156	434	4676	727
	BMEOs returning data	33	36	6	71	21
Hours per volunteer	Mean number per BMEO	6.0	8.0	7.9	7.4	5.2
	BMEOs returning data	31	35	6	69	20

Generally, BMEOs offer only a limited range of facilities. There was no firm link between size of organisation or organisational status, and the type of facility offered; or between the type of facility and the ethnic group served.

BMEOs offering general information and advice tended to have a room in an office or house. A natural extension of this role consists of 'making referrals' and 'helping to access the services provided by mainstream agencies'. In terms of premises and equipment, a conveniently located and accessible office with, perhaps, private areas for individual counselling and some administrative space seems to be the basic requirement for providing a simple advisory service.

According to the literature on black and minority ethnic organisations,[30] large numbers take education and train-

Table 8 *Origins by size and legal status of organisation (percentage of each size band or legal status)*

How established	Income band			Legal status	
	Up to £50k	*£50– £249k*	*Over £250k*	*Formal*	*Informal*
As a self-help group	61.3	55.2	31.3	47.6	61.7
By a particular minority community	58.1	70.7	68.8	69.8	42.6
By residents of a particular neighbourhood	11.3	12.1	6.3	11.9	10.6
By individuals with shared interests	50.0	24.1	37.5	33.3	53.2
By existing mainstream organisation	6.5	5.2	6.3	6.3	6.4
By existing BME organisation or group, primarily to serve non-members	11.3	13.8	6.3	10.3	8.5
Number	62	58	16	126	47

ing very seriously; our survey confirms this. About two-thirds of the larger organisations, over half of the medium-sized, and nearly a quarter of the smaller ones provide in-house courses. Half of the medium-sized to large organisations also run courses using outside staff. The provision of access to externally run courses is not quite as great but, even here, over 20 per cent of medium-sized and nearly a third of large organisations provide such access.

Although only a small number of BMEOs overall (4 per cent of small organisations, and 11 per cent of medium-sized ones) offer residential facilities, this rises to 50 per cent of the larger organisations. Hostels for young people, battered wives, or those who are

mentally disturbed, sheltered accommodation for elderly people, and those who are physically distressed, are therefore not beyond the reach of BMEOs. However, they are likely to be particularly associated with the housing associations.

As for premises, nearly a third (29 per cent) of all BMEOs rented office space, while nearly a quarter (22.5 per cent) owned their own accommodation. However, ownership was most common among the larger BMEOs, with 40 per cent of the largest BMEOs and 25 per cent of the medium-sized owning their own premises. Thirty-three per cent of the largest and 43.3 per cent of the medium-sized BMEOs rented accommodation. The other major tenure for the

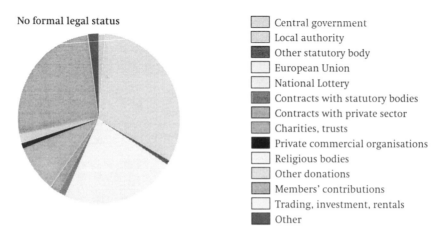

No formal legal status

- Central government
- Local authority
- Other statutory body
- European Union
- National Lottery
- Contracts with statutory bodies
- Contracts with private sector
- Charities, trusts
- Private commercial organisations
- Religious bodies
- Other donations
- Members' contributions
- Trading, investment, rentals
- Other

Figure 7 *Main sources of BMEO funding for all BMEOs with no formal legal status (slices represent percentages of all funding)*

largest BMEOs was provision of space by statutory agencies.

Many of the smallest BMEOs were housed in a private residence (30.2 per cent), although about a sixth (in each case) owned or rented their accommodation. The other most common arrangement was sharing a community centre or being provided with space by a voluntary body. A small number (3.2 per cent) had no physical base at all.

BMEOs with no formal legal status were most likely to share a community centre (23.4 per cent) or to be based in a private residence (21.3 per cent), though 12.8 per cent (in each case) owned or rented their accommodation.

Three-quarters of all BMEOs who owned their own accommodation have properties worth £50,000 or more. The largest organisations were most likely to own the most valuable property – for over half of these, it was worth more than £250,000. There is relatively little

difference between the small and medium-sized BMEOs on this score, though there were twice as many smaller organisations owning property worth less than £15,000 than medium-sized organisations.

This pattern is also revealed in regard to legal status, with informal organisations more likely to own less valuable property. The value of property owned by BMEOs is undoubtedly influenced by the high general property prices in many of the areas in which people from minority ethnic groups are concentrated (such as London boroughs).

Provident and friendly societies had the highest valued properties. These include some of the housing associations. More than half of them own their own premises, and a further quarter have arrangements not specified in our questionnaire (probably stock transfer agreements with larger housing associations). The BMEOs most likely not

Table 9 *Legal status and funding source (percentage distribution of funding by source)*

	Formal	Informal	Formal	Informal	Per cent of all funding going to informal organisations
Central government	889,685	4000	2.5	1.2	0.4
Local authority	2,883,005	108,672	8.2	31.7	3.6
Other statutory body	1,470,412	3185	4.2	0.9	0.2
European Union	424,162	4250	1.2	1.2	1.0
National Lottery	1,762,058	74,040	5.0	21.6	4.0
Contracts with statutory bodies	1,103,880	4760	3.1	1.4	0.4
Contracts with private sector	188,215	6800	0.5	2.0	3.5
Charities, trusts	1,320,453	31,724	3.8	9.2	2.3
Private commercial organisations	97,452	3400	0.3	1.0	3.4
Religious bodies	7100	250	0.0	0.1	3.4
Other donations	369,479	6175	1.1	1.8	1.6
Members' contributions	399,755	88,618	1.1	25.8	18.1
Trading, investment, rentals	21,741,574		62.0	0.0	0.0
Other	2,401,747	7145	6.9	21.1	0.3
Sum of all sources	35,058,976	343,019	100.0	100.0	1.0

to own property at all are the 'non-formal' ones. This is not particularly surprising given that a lack of formal status would tend to preclude any clear title to property at the group level.

It is apparent that those BMEOs responding to our questionnaire show a significant level of property ownership. Some, at least, have a strong basis for sustainability in terms of providing advice and advocacy related facilities on their own premises (although we did not ask about mortgage repayments). We are also assuming these properties are reasonably accessible to the community.

Discussion with BMEO representatives in our case studies further clarified attitudes towards ownership. One, on being asked whether the sharing of joint facilities would ease the resource burden, stated:

No, that's what the council has been trying to get us to do for years – mergers.

Table 10 *Percentage of organisations providing facilities*

Facilities provided	Income band				Legal status	
	Up to £50k	£50–£249k	Over £250k	All	Formal	Informal
Advice and information (general, public)	73.8	87.1	81.3	80.4	86.1	63.8
Assessment and/or referral services	33.8	72.6	75.0	55.2	57.7	38.3
Individual client counselling	38.5	69.4	75.0	55.9	60.6	29.8
Mentoring programmes	16.9	14.5	18.8	16.1	16.1	12.8
Consultancy and/or technical support	9.2	6.5	43.8	11.9	10.2	8.5
Access to specialised services provided by other agencies	32.3	62.9	62.5	49.0	50.4	34.0
'Outreach' support (including home visits)	40.0	71.0	75.0	57.3	59.9	36.2
In-house educational and/or training courses provided by your own staff and volunteers	23.1	54.8	62.5	41.3	46.0	21.3
Education or training provided on your premises by staff from other organisations	15.4	40.3	50.0	30.1	35.0	17.0
Access to external education and training courses	13.8	21.0	31.3	18.9	19.0	17.0
Day-care facilities (eg drop-in centre)	21.5	40.3	25.0	30.1	33.6	17.0
Dining facilities (eg lunch club or similar)	21.5	21.0	18.8	21.0	20.4	12.8
Transportation facilities (eg for trips, outings and visits)	21.5	25.8	31.3	24.5	26.3	19.1
Residential facilities (eg hostel, home)	4.6	11.3	50.0	12.6	13.9	4.3
Facilities for artistic and cultural events	35.4	33.9	25.0	33.6	32.1	34.0
Recreation, sports and leisure facilities	24.6	24.2	6.3	22.4	19.0	29.8
Meeting room or managed workspace facilities	16.9	29.0	18.8	22.4	25.5	10.6

Table 10 *continued*

Facilities provided	Income band				Legal status	
	Up to £50k	£50–£249k	Over £250k	All	Formal	Informal
Resource centre, library or research facilities	10.8	25.8	18.8	18.2	21.9	10.6
Information exchange facilities	43.1	51.6	56.3	48.3	46.7	38.3
Interpretation facilities	41.5	40.3	43.8	41.3	40.1	36.2
Other facilities	16.9	21.0	18.8	18.9	19.7	25.5
All	65	62	16	143	137	47

Squeeze us into one little spot and then cut down on the budget they have to spend on us. We took the decision to acquire our own property, so that we would have some independence – anyone else with sense did the same thing. We don't need the local authority to survive – we've got our own bookshop and we've built our own hostel. I suppose for groups just starting out sharing facilities would be all right, but not if you want to survive in the long run.

Many felt that for most established organisations, owning your own place was the ultimate aspiration, even if this meant being cautious about working too closely with other BMEOs which 'might swallow you up'.

Forty per cent of organisations responding to the postal survey use rented office space. However, the larger ones were more likely to be sharing space in a community centre, with 10 per cent actually owning their own centre and another 8 per cent working from space provided by a statutory agency.

The biggest users of rented office space are, in fact, companies limited by guarantee (roughly half of them). Organisations serving 'other BME' beneficiaries are the least likely to rent. This may be because groups classified as 'other BME' cover more recent arrivals (such as Yemenis, Moroccans etc), including refugees. Some organisations are buying hostels or small hotels to house them.

The Birmingham case study discussions confirmed that companies limited by guarantee were the ones most likely to have been set up under the auspices of a local authority or TEC, specifically for the purposes of receiving a grant. Grants usually covered renting space – in some cases, on property owned by the city council. Some concern was expressed, however, (particularly by organisations that owned their own property), that 'money for the black community' was being used to 'make someone from another community rich'. Furthermore, the office space rented was rarely located in the heart of the

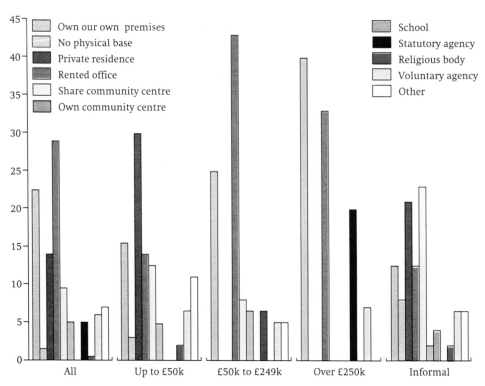

Figure 8 *BMEOs – access to premises (percentage of organisations)*

community. This contributed to an outflow of resources from the areas that could most do with the further development of commercial opportunities.

Non-formal or 'other status' organisations (20–25 per cent) are most inclined to make use of space in community centres. The rest operate from private residences (non-formals) or have no physical base ('other status'). Community centres are most used by organisations serving the Chinese and Indian communities. The latter, along with organisations serving 'other BME' beneficiaries, are also the ones most likely to own their community centre.

It is clear therefore that some BMEOs do benefit from shared facilities provided under the auspices of a community centre, and that some community centres (mainly ethnic associations, such as centres for the Bangladeshi or Indian community) are actually owned by BMEOs. We identified several parts of the country where this type of arrangement appeared to be common. Establishing whether these shared facility arrangements help to improve BMEO sustainability was, however, beyond the scope of the study. This would be an interesting area for further research.

We also paid some attention to ethnicity, to establish whether BMEOs serving particular communities were more inclined to build up their own property base.

Table 11 *Value of property owned (percentage of BMEOs owning property)*

	Up to £50k	£50–£249k	Over £250k	All	Formal	Informal
Less than £15,000	26.3	11.1	0.0	15.9	13.6	20.0
£16,000–£49,000	15.8	16.7	0.0	13.6	15.9	0.0
£50,000–£99,000	15.8	22.2	28.6	20.5	20.5	30.0
£100,000–£249,000	21.1	22.2	14.3	20.5	20.5	50.0
More than £250,000	21.1	27.8	57.1	29.5	29.5	0.0
Number owning their own accommodation	19	18	7	44	44	10

Half of all organisations serving the Bangladeshi community own their own premises, as do significant numbers of those serving the Pakistani, Indian and 'other BME' communities. The property owned by these groups, however, is much more likely to fall within the lower property value range.

Organisations serving people from African or Caribbean backgrounds are least likely to be owners (and, in the Caribbean case, even when they are, the properties are of low value). Forty per cent rent office space (rising to two-thirds for those serving Africans), while the rest are inclined to operate from a private residence or from a space provided by a voluntary or religious body, or community centre.

We could put this crudely by saying that Asian-oriented organisations tend to be 'owners' and African Caribbean organisations 'renters', although the property of the former is of low value. Any general stereotyping around this issue, however, is likely to be confounded by the fact that African, Caribbean and Asian-led BMEOs are all featured among the organisations owning the most highly valued properties.

Also of interest is the high level of ownership among organisations serving 'other BME' communities – which include refugees and asylum seekers. It would be useful to know whether such groups are already beginning to develop welfare-related services centred on the purchase of relevant properties.

Equipment

BMEOs' possession of equipment shows a clearer pattern than does ownership of property.

The organisations with no legal status generally have less than £5,000 worth of equipment, and those of 'other' status, less than £15,000. Charities were evenly spread throughout the range of up to £30,000. Companies limited by guarantee have equipment ranging up to the value of £100,000, but lie mainly in the range of £5,000 to £15,000. Provident and

Table 12 *Number of organisations whose main physical base for operations was a rented office*

Main ethnic group served	Income band			Total	Legal status	
	Up to £50k	£50–£249k	Over £250k		Formal	Informal
African	3	2	2	7	10	
Caribbean	1	4		5	4	1
Pakistani	1	1		2	4	
Bangladeshi		2		2	4	
Indian	1	2	1	4	5	2
Chinese		1		1	2	
Other BME	1	1		2	2	
From all BME groups	1	7	1	9	9	1
From all ethnic groups	1	6	1	8	9	2
Total	9	26	5	40	47	6

friendly societies show an interesting dichotomy. More than 40 per cent possessed less than £5,000 worth of equipment, although about one third had equipment worth £10,000 or more.

It is here that the connection between the status of the organisation and its asset base is at its clearest. Provident and friendly societies comprise both the large housing associations and smaller, welfare-oriented, ethnic associations. Charities tend to be larger ethnic associations, and companies limited by guarantee are usually the recipients of local authority or other funds connected with the delivery of a specific type of service on a local scale.

To summarise, BMEOs, of all size and shape, exhibit a surprisingly high level of property ownership, although much of this is of a low value type. In the case of some organisations, however, particu-larly the housing associations, the property values are significant. Bearing in mind the main types of service that these organisations provide, the physical basis for these BMEOs appears to be relatively sustainable in the medium-term. They generally do not make much of a call on specialised equipment and can be run from a variety of premises.

BMEO 'renters', however, are likely to be much more dependent on obtaining funds from external sources to maintain the physical basis of their operations. This applies particularly to those serving the African and Caribbean communities, whatever their income band or legal status.

If funding (or, alternatively, the free provision of space) is not forthcoming from mainstream agencies, it is hard to see a way in which BMEOs will be able to maintain a physical presence in the

---

Property Acquisition Case Study: Brent Indian Association

Mr Jagdish Patel, the manager of the Brent Indian Association, was concerned
that the council had terminated the operation of the local Citizens' Advice
Bureau (CAB), a move he believes was only made possible because of the services
provided by the Association, which had no resources from the Council. The
advice service had proved to be very much in demand, and demand had
increased since the closure of the CAB.

The Association applied to the council for funding to set up a drop-in centre,
for which there was ample evidence of demand. The Association intended to
build an extension to the current building housing the organisation. However,
there was also a need to renovate the building, which was in a state of disrepair.
The funding application was refused, with, Mr Patel felt, no real reason being
given.

The Association had managed, however, to acquire the ownership of the building for only £18,000. Prior to purchase, a 'peppercorn' rent had been paid and
the Association also had a long-term lease for the land on which the building
stood. All of this had stood them in good stead when it came to negotiating the
purchase.

Mr Patel feels that help and support from the council has been, and remains,
absolutely minimal. In real terms, most of the inroads that have been made came
via help from the local temples and shopkeepers in the area.

---

communities they serve. The only option
may be, as in the case of the smaller and
less well established non-formal BMEOs,
to operate from pubs or from one
another's homes.

The case study below shows how
vulnerable some BMEOs can feel, particularly when they have access to only
minimal council funding.

Staffing and volunteers

Another key sustainability issue is
whether BMEOs can attract the right
kind of staff and volunteers, and in

sufficient quantities. Almost half of the
postal survey respondents employed
between four and seven staff, with the
rest employing over eight (28 per cent)
or between one and three (23 per cent).

Only a quarter of the total BME
workforce comprises full-time male staff
(part-time males make up another 12 per
cent). Sixty-one per cent of the workforce
is female, just under half of these being
part-timers.

In the largest organisations, over 80
per cent of employees work full-time,
though medium-sized BMEOs are more
likely than small BMEOs to employ part-

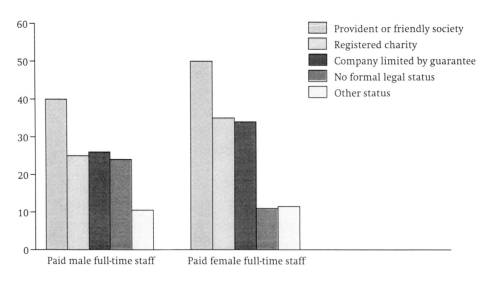

Figure 9 *Male and female workforce by type of organisation (percentage of staff in each type of organisation)*

timers. The position is almost completely reversed for BMEOs with no formal legal status, with only a fifth of their employees working full-time.

The percentage of full-time male staff is highest in the provident and friendly societies, whereas the percentage of male part timers is highest for the non-formal and 'other status' BMEOs.

The percentage of staff in the case who are full-time females is again highest in the provident and friendlies, followed, as with full-time males, by charities and the companies limited by guarantee. The highest percentage of female staff is in the non-formal or 'other status' organisations.

Full-timers, in other words, whether male or female, tend to be working with the larger and better-resourced BMEOs. The smaller and less formal organisations have to rely on part-time staff, the vast majority of whom are women.

Qualifications

Although not the only indicator, the level of qualifications does give some idea of the quality of the staff employed in an organisation and, in turn, the potential level of productivity in an organisation and long-term efficiency. Our findings revealed that the standard of qualifications was probably higher than most people would imagine.

More than half of all BMEO staff possess graduate or postgraduate qualifications, with a further sixth having professional qualifications of one sort or another. Qualifications are highest in the larger organisations and in those serving 'all black and minority ethnic groups', 'all ethnic groups' and 'other BME groups'. The percentage is lowest for organisations serving the Caribbean, Chinese and Bangladeshi ethnic groups.

Table 13 *Percentage of BMEO staff with formal qualifications*

	Up to £50k	£50–£249k	Over £250k	All	Formal	Informal
No post-school qualifications	9.4	10.4	3.6	7.7	7.9	24.4
NVQ1 or 2 equivalent	3.1	10.7	8.6	7.9	8.4	3.3
NVQ3 or equivalent	9.4	15.0	21.3	15.7	14.7	11.1
First degree or equivalent	56.1	27.5	43.3	40.9	40.2	31.1
Post-graduate qualifications	9.0	13.3	12.2	11.8	12.0	16.7
Professional qualifications	12.9	23.1	11.0	16.0	16.8	13.3
All staff	100.0	100.0	100.0	100.0	100.0	100.0

In general, BMEO staff could be said to be very well qualified.

The percentage of graduate staff is highest in the smallest BMEOs, but a quarter of the staff of BMEOs with no formal legal status have no post-school qualifications. Those with postgraduate qualifications are most common in the medium-sized and larger organisations. Nearly a quarter (23.1 per cent) of the staff of medium-sized BMEOs hold professional qualifications.

Despite the predominance of a female workforce, the research indicates that the person responsible for coordinating BMEO activities on a day to day basis is most likely to be a man. He is likely to be a fairly well qualified, 25 to 45-year-old, and with past experience in the voluntary sector. But he is less likely actually to be sitting on the management committee of the BMEO he is running. Women are more likely to be running smaller BMEs (but not those with no formal legal status). Levels of qualification among managers increase with size of organisation. Managers of small and informal BMEOs are least likely to have experience elsewhere and are least likely to be paid. Very few managers are aged under 25 and older managers are most common in the largest BMEOs.

We asked BMEOs about any difficulties they had in recruiting or retaining staff. The main reasons given for any such difficulties were that pay and career prospects were better outside the voluntary sector as a whole (that is, not just outside BMEOs). This was particularly relevant for companies limited by guarantee and for organisations catering to African and Caribbean-oriented BMEOs.

Table 14 *Characteristics of manager/coordinator (percentage of each type of BMEO)*

	Up to £50k	£50–£249k	Over £250k	All	Formal	Informal
Is on the management committee (or equivalent)	52.8	22.2	26.7	35.1	36.6	50.0
Is paid	24.5	93.7	100.0	66.4	71.8	28.1
Is from the BME community	47.2	79.4	93.3	67.9	70.2	53.1
Is female	45.3	44.4	20.0	42.0	44.3	34.4
Has postgraduate degree	24.5	30.2	40.0	29.0	29.8	37.5
Has first degree	32.1	33.3	53.3	35.1	36.6	31.3
Has professional qualifications	49.1	57.1	33.3	51.1	53.4	40.6
Has experience in local authority	28.3	38.1	26.7	32.8	32.1	34.4
Has experience in other statutory body	13.2	20.6	33.3	19.1	24.4	12.5
Has experience in BME voluntary sector	34.0	49.2	73.3	45.8	48.1	31.3
Has experience in mainstream voluntary sector	22.6	33.3	40.0	29.8	30.5	18.8
Has experience in commercial organisation	15.1	28.6	33.3	23.7	22.9	18.8
Has experience in trade or business association	9.4	19.0	13.3	14.5	13.0	18.8
Is aged below 25	5.7	1.6	0.0	3.1	2.3	3.1
Is aged 25–44	49.1	55.6	40.0	51.1	49.6	53.1
Is aged above 45	50.9	46.0	60.0	49.6	51.1	46.9
All	53	63	15	131	131	32

Volunteers

On the volunteer side, BMEOs may, on average, draw upon ten volunteers in a typical week. These will be more or less evenly divided between men and women, but the women will contribute roughly 15 hours a week more than men, volunteering on average for more than 40 hours per week (see Table 15 below).

The number of hours contributed tends to be greatest for companies

Table 15 *Contribution of volunteers (percentage of all volunteers in each type of BMEO)*

	Up to £50k	£50– £249k	Over £250k	All	Formal	Informal
Young unemployed	5.2	10.3	17.5	9.1	9.5	8.2
Adult unemployed	12.0	30.6	32.7	24.2	25.1	10.2
Retired	21.3	15.6	4.8	16.7	15.8	16.3
Students	6.9	10.7	9.5	9.3	9.3	9.3
Parents with young children	4.7	1.5	11.3	3.5	4.2	7.7
Religious workers	4.9	1.5	0.0	2.5	2.5	1.1
Employed persons	39.0	27.2	22.1	30.9	30.9	40.5
Other	6.1	2.6	2.1	3.8	2.7	6.8
Total number of volunteers	255	407	62	724	716	147

limited by guarantee and registered charities, and for organisations serving the 'other BME' and African ethnic groups.

Unemployed people are more likely to work as volunteers for larger BMEOs. Smaller and informal organisations draw more heavily upon people in work.

In the LOVAS Smethwick study, the mean number of volunteers per organisation was 27.2, the mean number of voluntary hours per organisation per week was 87.5, and the mean number of hours per volunteer per week was 4.9. The majority of voluntary organisations and about half of community groups had no minority ethnic volunteers at all. But 14 per cent of the voluntary organisations had a volunteer force where 50 per cent or more were from an ethnic minority. It is probable that many of these were BMEOs.

The 1991 National Survey on Voluntary Activity in the UK found only a 2.5 per cent rate of black volunteering, as compared with an overall national rate of 5.5 per cent. This would appear to indicate that people from the minority ethnic communities were less likely to volunteer, but this might be a misconception.

In the organisations in our survey, although retired people make a significant contribution to BMEO provision, especially to those serving the Caribbean community, the most plentiful source of volunteers is adults of working age, both in and out of employment.

Unemployed adults are most likely to volunteer to be used by companies limited by guarantee and those constituted as charities. Those who are otherwise employed are more likely to work for provident and friendly societies, or in non-formal and 'other status' BMEOs. They are especially likely to be volunteering for organisations serving Bangladeshis, but are common in organisations serving every type of community – with the exception of African and 'other' BME communities. Discussions with community organisations as part of our case studies indicated that employed people are more likely to be serving as management committee members, technical advisors, or mentors.

Unemployed young people are more likely to be found in organisations serving the 'other BME', African and Pakistani communities. Students are a particularly important source of volunteers for organisations serving the Chinese community.

In minority communities, leisure-based social activities, education-focused activities, religious and cultural activities tend to revolve around building a sense of cultural identity and pride – particularly among disaffected young people:

> *Much of the volunteering done by the black community tends to take place within the community itself, through churches, temples, mosques, community groups and professional and welfare organisations. This volunteering is very often made necessary by the inappropriateness of the services offered by other voluntary organisations or by the local authority – services that do not meet the specific needs of the Black community.*[31]

A survey of black and minority young people[32] suggested that the issue revolved around the fact that two-thirds

of them had no particular preference with respect to the type of organisation they volunteered for. Only 10 per cent had an image of volunteering as a middle class activity. Time, financial worries (for example, the effect on benefits) and lack of information were the main barriers to volunteering.

In the Smethwick study, 40 per cent of organisations reported that recruitment of volunteers was getting harder. A similar picture emerged from our survey – 37 per cent stated that recruiting volunteers had become more difficult in the past two years, compared to just 6 per cent who felt it had become easier. Those serving the Caribbean and Bangladeshi communities are particularly likely to have experienced difficulties.

Retaining volunteers is less of a problem, but, nonetheless, for at least 30 per cent of BMEOs it has become more difficult. In the Smethwick study, the figure was just over 25 per cent. Those serving the Chinese, Bangladeshi or African communities are the hardest hit.

In conclusion, it seems likely that BMEO staffing issues will become an increasingly important sustainability issue in the years to come, but only, perhaps, for organisations dealing with specific minority ethnic communities. In the case of volunteers, some minority ethnic communities may face increasing problems with getting younger people to contribute to BMEO activities.

Growth constraints and development needs

Constraints

The LOVAS survey of Smethwick provides a guide to the main growth issues facing voluntary and community groups as a whole. For voluntary organisations, the biggest problems were (in order of importance):

1. obtaining sufficient funds;
2. raising funds for capital projects; and
3. recruiting volunteers.

For community groups, volunteer recruitment was the most frequently reported problem, followed by obtaining sufficient funds and having enough active members.

Funding issues were perceived by all the formal organisations we surveyed, whatever their size, to be the biggest constraint to growth. (See Figure 13.) They emphatically placed 'lack of easily accessible funding' at the top of their list regardless of ethnic group served. (The term 'accessible' had been used in order to differentiate between those circumstances where no funding was available for a particular type of service, and those for which funding was apparently available, but could not be accessed.)

Non-formal organisations, however, not unnaturally saw 'lack of official recognition' as the key issue. For the 'other status' organisations, lack of space was the problem. Both types of organisation, however, placed lack of accessible funding as their number two concern.

Lack of funding geared specifically to the services provided was the second most important constraint – suggesting that funding geared towards advocacy and advice might be harder to obtain than funding for more precisely defined 'deliverables'. Again, the particular ethnic group served made no difference to the ranking.

The third most frequently mentioned item, lack of knowledge of what funding opportunities might be available, is, perhaps, an indication of the isolation of these organisations from mainstream, including statutory, resource networks. It may be, for example, that specialist fundraisers could help them to overcome this constraint. Organisations serving Pakistani, African and Caribbean communities were particularly likely to see this as a problem.

Our case study discussions with minority-led organisations about 'accessible' funding brought out the following views:

- Accessing core funding, rather than funding for the delivery of specific services, was becoming more difficult.
- Although many programmes stressed the inclusion of ethnic minority communities, few were specifically targeted at areas with the highest ethnic minority population levels. Even when programmes applied to

specific wards, the way boundaries were drawn could mean that only part of the ethnic minority community of a particular area could be included in the programme.

- The paperwork involved in SRB and similar bids was excessive from the point of view of small organisations, particularly when it involved the development of a 'business plan'.
- Only the larger BMEOs have had any sort of experience with developing such plans, and for smaller organisations, the cost of hiring outside consultancy help was prohibitive. This issue was exacerbated by the fact that different programmes require different business plan formats.
- The current emphasis on wide-ranging partnerships places BMEOs at a disadvantage in developing 'black-led' bids. Potential partners are much bigger and better resourced organisations who want BMEOs to 'fit in with their plans' rather than take a lead role.
- The current emphasis on fitting in with local and regional development plans puts BMEOs at a disadvantage because they are less well placed than others to know the whys and wherefores of such planning.
- The semi-privatisation of agencies such as TECs allows for too much 'top-slicing' of funds intended to benefit the black community. Some expressed their suspicions that these organisations applied for, and received, 'ethnic minority funding' but used a significant part of this to

fund their own operations, rather than passing it on to BMEOs.

This was compounded by a feeling that funding is moving away from 'black-only' to 'multi-cultural' uses. More and more white-led organisations were competing for these funds. One person interviewed said:

> White-led organisations see the African Caribbean community as a market, especially in the care sector. They are prepared to provide services to African Caribbeans as an appendage to their normal services and funders go to them.

Our case study indicated that smaller and newly established BMEOs often had difficulties with meeting the 'track record' and quality standards associated with mainstream funding programmes. These had been developed for well established mainstream agencies and were not seen as particularly relevant to the operations of community-based groups. There was an expressed desire for standards appropriate either to small community organisations and/or minority-led organisations. There was a feeling that the situation might worsen with the creation of new mainstream organisations as a result of shake-ups of many policy areas and funding sources.

Lack of official recognition was a relatively significant restraint, not just for non-formal organisations, but also for both provident and friendly societies, and companies limited by guarantee. This is surprising, because both types of grouping contain some of the largest and most well established BMEOs. Organisations serving Chinese, Indian and 'other BME' communities were particularly affected.

Lack of space and facilities was also given a relatively high rating by provident and friendly societies and was seen as the number one constraint by 'other status' organisations.

Issues connected with volunteers were given a relatively low ranking, with only non-formal organisations perceiving it as being particularly significant (ranked second). In light of the Smethwick findings, it suggests that these informal groups are closer to being community groups in the 'LOVAS' sense (ie, ones dealing in community self-help, rather than having a philanthropy to those in need).

Capacity building needs

Capacity building has, in recent years, been trumpeted almost as a panacea for BMEOs and for the community and voluntary sector in general. Although a widely used term, it is, however, poorly understood and implemented.

We define it in this report in its more limited sense – as developing an organisation so that it can provide a better service to the people it currently serves and gradually extend and diversify its services to others.

However, capacity building can ultimately be seen to be about building the capacity of deprived communities and individuals within those communi-

ties to improve the quality of their lives.

A particularly good definition of capacity building is:

> *a comprehensive process which includes the ability to identify constraints and to plan and manage development. Ideally, it aims at improving on existing capabilities and resources and using them efficiently to achieve sustainable economic and social development.*[33]

In exploring how capacity building could be carried out in a way that adds to BMEO sustainability, the Deakin Report of the Commission on the Future of the Voluntary Sector provides a convenient summary of one of the key issues:

> *A variety of views were expressed about the ways of developing black and ethnic minority voluntary organisations. Some felt the answer lay with the wider voluntary sector – encourage more joint ventures (Guide Association), more support from larger, mainstream organisations (Voluntary Arts Network). Others felt that funders should play a more pro-active role (Association of Charitable Foundations, GLAD, Millfield House).*[34]

Burridge,[35] in arguing that voluntary service councils are an efficient and effective way of supporting local voluntary organisations, pinpoints a few simple but important ways in which they could help provide:

- access to resources and facilities (meeting rooms, telephones, transportation);
- information and training on fundraising and legal matters;
- finding a few paid workers in order to support more volunteers ;
- help with book-keeping; and
- help with evaluating work.

He also points out, however, that some community voices, including those of black people, were still not being heard, and that they would need additional information and support, even in getting a hearing at the local voluntary services council.

The BMEOs we interviewed were asked about their development or capacity building needs and how they could be met. Help with grant applications, general fund raising and sponsorship were the clear priorities. These were followed by help with developing project or business plans. Both of these are obviously related to the growth constraints associated with lack of access to funding.

Help with recruiting and training volunteers was the item most frequently ranked third as a capacity building need, but this was strongly influenced by two particular types of organisation – provident and friendly societies, and 'other status' organisations. This was probably because both types of organisation trade on an image of professionalism, business-like conduct and links with the mainstream. People with the appropriate skills would probably expect to get paid

by these organisations, rather than act as volunteers.

BMEOs serving the Bangladeshi, Chinese and 'other BME' communities were also the most affected. Chinese organisations we spoke to seemed to find students used to be a good source of volunteers, but this is becoming less the case.

Interestingly, only companies limited by guarantee and 'other status' BMEOs perceived staff or volunteer training to be a growth constraint. Provident and friendly societies did not. It is likely that the latter are facing constraints on finding younger recruits to act as volunteers, as our discussions with one Chinese organisation suggest. According to the Coventry Chinese Community Organisation, Chinese students are more inclined to get involved in mainstream activities than they used to be and are thus less likely to be readily available for voluntary work in the community.

Help with grant applications was seen as the most important capacity building action by small and medium-sized BMEOs, while medium-sized organisations were also concerned about obtaining suitable accommodation. Small organisations mentioned their need for support in managing a voluntary organisation.

In the qualitative study, we asked BMEOs whether the local mainstream voluntary sector infrastructure could provide greater access to capacity building resources, thereby adding to their sustainability. Opinions were divided. One argument, generally put forward by the larger organisations, was that Voluntary Service Councils (VSCs) have traditionally had little contact with the black communities, and have made little effort to include them in their programmes; they have rarely even employed black staff. It is only since funding has become tight that they have shown an interest – and they have done this by putting in bids with an ethnic minority element. This helps to cover their overheads, but does not necessarily contribute to black community development. All too often this community is not properly consulted when the bids are put in. VSCs, it is argued, are in fact competing for funds with BMEOs.

A second, more benign view was put forward by some of the smaller organisations. VSCs were perceived as having access to networks and resources which are far beyond the reach of small, black-led groups. By participating in their programmes, BMEOs can keep abreast of what is going on, network with white-led organisations sharing similar interests, and gain practical skills in areas such as book-keeping and managing a voluntary organisation.

4. Relationship to Mainstream Agencies

The interviews with mainstream agencies

We wanted to assess both the attitude towards BMEOs of mainstream agencies and the extent to which their explicit policies towards BMEOs (if any existed) were affecting the development of BMEOs.

As most mainstream organisations do not have a policy of targeting BMEOs *per se*, there is not much evidence of their rigorously monitoring or evaluating the role that BMEOs play in helping them to deliver their objectives. Our research has had to rely on subjective views of senior officers, and on analysing grants data in published documents, based on our knowledge of which organisations were BMEOs.

We held semi-structured interviews with 50 mainstream agencies and other resource providers in the two case study areas of Soho and Handsworth, Birmingham, and Brent, London. The purpose of this part of the research was to obtain an overview of:

- the policy (explicit and implicit) and practice of these organisations with regard to BMEOs;
- the factors that influence this policy and practice;

- the type and size of resource flows to BMEOs; and
- mainstream organisations' views on the importance of BMEOs, their needs and the factors most important for their sustainability, including the likely levels of future support.

We interviewed senior managers from a wide range of organisations across the whole spectrum of social and economic policy, including:

- local authority departments (BMEO support tends to operate through several local authority departments rather than being a purely corporate function);
- local branches of central government and quasi-public sector agencies such as TECs;
- regional organisations such as government regional offices, Housing Corporation regional offices and Regional Development Agencies;
- local and regional voluntary organi-sations which provide support to local BMEOs; and
- national support and funding agencies such as the National Lottery Charities Board, the Black Training and Enterprise Group (a black organi-sation that promotes training,

employment and enterprise policies that benefit black people) and Project Fullemploy.

A list of organisations interviewed is contained in Appendix II.

The determinants of policy and practice

Our research suggests that at present the policy of most agencies is primarily influenced by two factors:

1. national policy on targeting black and minority ethnic people and BMEOs through their particular thematic area of operation (for example, housing, health, training); and
2. local partnerships and local pressures.

There was little evidence that the Home Office's Voluntary Sector Compact,[36] introduced in 1998, was having an impact at the time of our research: the majority of people interviewed were not familiar with it. However, Government Offices for the Regions are currently developing regional frameworks for the voluntary sector as a whole, using government social exclusion statements to drive forward change. Key areas of local government are also taking action. For example, Birmingham City Council's Central Policy Unit is preparing local versions of the compact.

These are positive moves which are likely to have some influence. However, the picture of policy formation and implementation provided by our interviews suggests that at present, the most effective drivers of change are likely to be reviews of thematic policies which explicitly address the role of BMEOs in reaching target groups, and the development of local partnerships with BMEO policies.

The social exclusion agenda, promoted by the government, appears to have had the effect of generating some rhetoric about 'voluntary sector inclusion', with most agencies now having a policy relating to this, although sometimes on a rather ad hoc basis. In addition, most agencies had, or were, developing policies to target the specific needs of individuals of BME origin, although written policies providing more detail than the widespread general equal opportunities policies were less in evidence.

When this research was undertaken, the impact of the MacPherson report on the handling of the investigation into the death of Stephen Lawrence had not had time to manifest itself in the form of formal written policies. However, a number of interviewees did refer to the existence of institutional racism and processes underway to develop policies to address this (for example, the fact there were no models of health care which were acceptable to black communities and the need to re-commission health services, using community based workers, to address this). Some SRB partnerships in London admitted that they did not do enough in early days to engage BMEOs and new bids were addressing this. However, the large majority of agencies interviewed did not have a specific BMEO component to their policy, and did not systematically monitor their relationship with BMEOs *per se*.

The most notable exception is the Registered Social Landlords (RSL) sector. The Housing Corporation has a policy of supporting black-led RSLs as part of its overall 'black and minority ethnic strategy', which is usually backed proactively by local authority housing departments and supported by other RSLs that provide a 'shelter' for smaller black-led RSLs.

This 'shelter' works in a number of ways. Larger RSLs may undertake the development of housing for black-led RSLs and pass the finished units over for them to manage. Eventually, ownership of the housing might be passed over to the black-led RSL. Other support may be: underwriting cashflow; mentoring and shadowing of staff; allowing access to training courses; and so on.

In this way, some larger RSLs in London have helped Ujima, now a large black-led RSL, reach the asset-based capacity to be fully independent. Support is also being provided to very small housing organisations which serve the needs of refugee communities.

In addition, some local authority departments explicitly encourage specific BMEOs within the implementation of their departmental programmes, such as economic development. In Birmingham, all departments have to produce 'equality action plans' to

explain how they will meet the needs of BME individuals. These sometimes make reference to the role of BMEOs in helping deliver these targets.

Regardless of the nature of the policy statements of the agencies interviewed, all of them expressed the conviction that BMEOs are needed to help them meet their objectives. The reasons given reflect the problems that agencies have had, not only in providing services to meet the needs of the minority ethnic population – not least because of a lack of understanding of these needs – but also with their ability to market their services to BME people.

A respondent from Birmingham Health Authority, for example, recognises that:

> ... we don't have the models of care that are acceptable to the black communities. We have to understand the enormity of the change that is needed – we have to work out how to re-commission the health service.

The approach of most mainstream agencies described here has resulted in a significant patchwork of supported BMEOs, providing a mix of services and advocacy, but a lack of a strategic approach that secures synergy between, and sustainability of, these BMEOs.

Types of engagement with BMEOs and resource flows

Resources flow to BMEOs from various public sector funds, some of which are

routed through quasi-public sector
bodies such as TECs. The range and
complexity of these sources of funding
are factors often mentioned in terms of
the capacity building needs of BMEOs.
They feel they need to be aware of, and
skilled at, accessing the myriad of funds.

Local authorities in the case study
areas remain major funders of BMEOs
and some of the grants they provide are
substantial in local terms (over £100,000
per year).[37] They also provide a wide
range of other types of support, such as
providing secondhand equipment or 'in-
kind' support, such as free access to
meeting facilities and help with
accounts, information provision, access
to central purchasing systems and access
to other funding and support networks.

Central government funds are routed
(often via regional development agencies
and regional government offices)
through bodies such as TECs, colleges,
health authorities, the probation
service, and the Employment Service. In
Birmingham, the Voluntary Sector
Council is also an important conduit of
these funds. In addition, funds are
allocated to partnerships of various
kinds, such as regeneration partnerships
and others formed to meet the requirements of specific funding regimes such
as health action zones, SureStart (an
initiative targeted at young children)
and education action zones.

Substantial funding, often worth
several million pounds (such as through
the European Social Fund (ESF) and
European Regional Development Fund
(ERDF)) is generated by Europe and,

again, the regional government office or
development agency. ESF and ERDF are
important conduits of support for
BMEOs, often via partnerships or local
authorities.

The possibilities in terms of what an
organisation can access are immense. But
both funding agencies and BMEOs say
that organisations need help to get
through the web of support that is available to them.

In general, agencies provide direct
funds to BMEOs by of one of the following:

- Output-driven formal contracts (the
  'contract culture') which is the
  method chosen by the TEC and
  Employment Service and which will
  not include a specific, core funding
  element.
- Service-level agreements (SLAs) which
  define the service to be provided for
  grant aid but are not strictly propor-
  tionate to output and can thus allow
  an element of core funding. The
  probation service and some
  departments of the local authority
  issue SLAs.
- General grant aid linked to the delivery of services or the performance of
  certain functions but without a tight
  specification of these services. These
  are most likely to contain a core
  funding element.

An interesting example of contractual
arrangements is that of the New Deal
(Welfare to Work), which is the responsibility of the Employment Service, who

first contract a local partnership. In Birmingham, for example, there is a joint venture partnership consisting of the Council, Chamber of Commerce, TEC and Voluntary Sector Council. This partnership, in turn, contracts with specific agencies, such as the TEC, to administer the contracts with providers. The TEC (or other agency) then contracts with a limited number of 'main contract holders', who in turn contract with smaller providers within their network.

For example, in Birmingham there are four main contract holders for the Gateway to New Deal, one of which, the Afro-Caribbean Resource Centre, is a BMEO. The main contract holders have subcontracts with smaller organisations, thus creating a network of New Deal providers.

By this mechanism, the TEC has limited the number of organisations it deals with directly. This allows the TECs to operate within their capacity but leaves little room for a strategic approach to capacity building and sustainability of BMEOs, pushing smaller organisations further down the chain. Instead, capacity building is contracted out to intermediaries.

There were differences among mainstream providers on the types of BMEOs they engaged with, which is often linked to the direct funding approach adopted. Some dealt with existing BMEOs that had been established for some time; others tended to create new BMEOs to deal with new policy issues; some relied on umbrella organisations or other partnerships rather than individual BMEOs. Grant-giving organisations tended to be more open to funding newer BMEOs.

Occasionally, mainstream organisations would deliver services directly while using BMEOs to advise on the form of their provision. For example, in the health arena, sickle cell organisations might give advice, black advisory committees might be set up to help business links and TECs, or ethnic minority forums might be set up as consultation mechanisms to assist local authorities.

Many of the agencies interviewed do not have the organisational capacity or strategic framework to allow them to interact directly with voluntary organisations, particularly the smaller organisations, many of which are BMEOs. Their strategy, as with the TEC described above, is to work with umbrella groups or to pass on resources at their disposal to partnership organisations (such as SRB programmes), main contract holders (such as New Deal), or intermediaries (such as the Birmingham Voluntary Sector Council (VSC)).

Advocacy and consultation arrangements

Consultation arrangements also differ, as do methods of obtaining information on needs of BMEOs. Some agencies have established methods of consultation with voluntary organisations in general and particularly with the organisations they support (for example, in Birmingham the West Midlands

Probation Service has a quarterly partnership forum held at Birmingham VSC). Others rely on umbrella groups to provide them with information, often providing funds to the umbrella groups specifically for this purpose. Still others have lists of BMEOs and other voluntary organisations which they write to or invite to consultation meetings on an ad hoc basis.

In the West Midlands, for example, the Government Office for the West Midlands Region, and Advantage West Midlands, the regional development agency for the West Midlands, have no formal consultation arrangements but refer to the SRB-funded Black Regeneration Network. This is a seven-year programme that has received £2m of SRB resources to provide BMEO capacity-building support, to establish a network of BMEOs active in the field of regeneration, and to be a regional advocate of the needs of BMEOs and the BME population.

At city level, Birmingham City Council has established 'Standing Consultative Forums' for specific minority ethnic communities. The Birmingham and Solihull TEC, by comparison, plans to use Birmingham Race Action Partnership as an umbrella body to give them feedback on the needs of BME communities, rather than trying to do the consultation directly themselves. It also funds Partnership for Change, an organisation that promotes the participation, achievement and progression of African Caribbeans in the city, and Birmingham VSC (BVSC), both of which help to keep it informed. The director of BVSC is on the TEC Board. The TEC believes that consultation is a strong point of their organisation, but it is clear that it does this through intermediaries and not directly with providers.

It is clearly important that BMEOs are in a position to influence decision makers. A health authority representative acknowledged this when speaking to us of the need to recommission the health service:

> ... the voluntary sector has to make sure that they're part of these debates – part of the planning – they have to keep knocking on the door.

There have been examples of BMEOs nudging agencies into taking the needs of black people on board. For example, the Black New Deal Partnership was formed in Birmingham when it became evident that there was under-representation of black groups in the New Deal programme. Changing institutional structures may make it harder to bring about changes. For instance, City College in Birmingham questioned how community organisations would be able to influence local learning and skills councils, as they would be established on a sub-regional basis.

Many of those interviewed stressed the importance of recognising the many differences within BME communities when consulting; not only ethnic differences, but also differences within specific ethnic groups.

Some interviewees emphasised the benefits of 'patch workers' in providing information on BME needs and the benefits of employing BME staff. This issue of gathering information on needs overlaps with the provision of development support.

Very little engagement takes place in terms of traditional community development activity (in other words, where community development professionals work on the ground directly with organisations, assisting them in the development of their organisations). Some departments of Birmingham City Council still attempt to undertake this work by using locally based officers for whom it is not their main job – for example, the youth service and some divisions of the housing department.

The health authority also uses its workers on the ground to provide intelligence. The Birmingham Voluntary Sector Council employs outreach development workers. The Employment Service used to have a team of outreach workers – inner-city officers – but funding ceased and they no longer undertake this type of work. Some area regeneration partnerships fund specific community project workers, whose role is to help develop voluntary and community organisations on their patch.

The role of partnerships and intermediaries

BMEOs receive significant support from organisations established specifically or partially to support the voluntary sector.

Most of these are voluntary organisations themselves.

In Birmingham, for example, BVSC is an important body in this respect. It is a large organisation that has a strong influence within the city, its director being on numerous boards and committees. It has gained substantial funding from sources such as SRB, European Social Fund, TEC and the city council to provide an extensive range of services for the voluntary sector, such as the PQASSO (Practical Quality Assurance System for Small Organisations) programme outlined above. Brent does not have the benefit of such an organisation. Brent did not have a Voluntary Sector Council and there was therefore no such vehicle available to provide similar support to voluntary and community organisations.

In most regions a number of black-led organisations have been established, often with a mission to support their communities, but which, in effect – and often by default – also support BME voluntary groups. In Birmingham, long-established organisations such as the Asian Resource Centre (which supports and mentors the Bangladeshi Youth Federation, for instance) and the Afro-Caribbean Resource Centre play this role, alongside newer organisations established specifically as umbrella groups, such as the Black Regeneration Network and the Birmingham Race Action Partnership.

Partnerships, such as those developed for administering SRB and other special funds, have also become important conduits of funds and support to BMEOs. Indeed, our interviews suggested that these have become increasingly important sources of funds for BMEOs in the two case study areas, replacing the old Inner City Partnership (Urban Programme) grants and, in some instances, mainstream funds.

Since Labour came into power there has been a growth of special funds again, which are supposed to be in addition to mainstream funds. However, there is suspicion among BMEOs that they are used sometimes to cut back on mainstream funds.

Capacity building and sustainability

Capacity building has been widely accepted as a significant need within the voluntary sector, enabling it to play a fuller and more effective role in civic society. In this context, a number of agencies have established programmes specifically for capacity building, based upon a variety of funding regimes, for example the European Social Fund, TEC and the Single Regeneration Budget.

Our research suggests that the further away that funding agencies are from day-to-day contact with voluntary organisations, the more likely they are to view capacity building in terms of their own needs rather than the needs of the voluntary organisations themselves. That is, they tend to be most interested in the capacity of organisations to respond to agencies' bureaucracy and administration. As one respondent put it:

The main needs of BME organisations are being able to deal with the paperwork and admin.

Another interviewee wanted BMEOs to:

... develop organising and scheduling skills, meet reporting requirements and produce accurate information on time – play by the rules. Be better able to carry out research, network, learn from others, allow themselves to be mentored, dismantle barriers.

BMEOs are expected to show:

... Adaptability. They must be assertive in the bidding process and prepared to accept advice. The rules and procedures apply to everybody and BME groups must learn to deal with this by following the guidance they are given. Afro-Caribbean groups have not been as successful as Asian groups in bids, and this probably stems from their unwillingness to accept the bureaucracy associated with applying.

In short, as one respondent put it:

They must learn to conform.

Most other agencies recognise that capacity building should be about helping BMEOs to deliver and develop services, but all stressed the need 'to be able to play the game' as a necessary survival skill, a lack of which is a weakness among many BMEOs.

In Birmingham, a rationalisation of the plethora of capacity-building programmes is beginning with the recognition of BVSC as a key provider of support through its PQASSO initiative. BVSC has received funds for this initiative from the city council, the TEC, SRB, and the European Social Fund (ESF).

PQASSO is not a quality system in the usual sense of the word, but is a comprehensive organisational development (and therefore capacity-building) tool which organisations implement themselves. The emphasis is on developing services or functions of the BMEO, rather than skills which are imparted separately from what the voluntary organisation does. For example, personnel management systems and skills would be looked at in the context of what the organisation actually does, rather than as an abstract set of principles. This is an important distinction, as many capacity-building programmes consist of generic skills training sessions rather than exercises related to the specific situation a BMEO finds itself in. Early on, a decision was taken to prioritise BMEOs for this support.

Most voluntary organisations and agencies agree that adequate core funding is the key sustainability need for BMEOs, yet this often appears to be forgotten in the newly discovered recognition of the importance of 'capacity building' in community development. While this is a welcome discovery, and one agency criticised grant giving without ensuring that the recipient had the capacity to use the grant,[38] there is a strong feeling among BMEOs that capacity building is being used as a substitute

for proper core funding.

Linked to this is a view of some agencies that funding should be backed by continual 'on the ground' support from community development or patch workers. This was contrasted with the approach of some grant givers who only contacted grant recipients for monitoring returns.

Few of the mainstream agencies raised the need to help BMEOs acquire income-generating capital assets as being a key contributor to their sustainability. But it was raised very strongly by some, particularly voluntary organisations supporting BMEOs. Within the housing association movement, obtaining an adequate capital base is viewed as essential for a black-led RSL to achieve long-term sustainability.

In the two case study areas, the local authority and the regional Housing Corporation office supported the acquisition of housing by black-led RSLs through a process of working closely with larger RSLs. The larger RSL will develop new housing with a smaller black-led RSL, passing over units for the latter to manage to begin with. The eventual aim is to pass over ownership of these units so that the black-led RSL eventually acquires the necessary critical mass of good quality housing stock to be sustainable.

White-led RSLs also provide training, seconding and mentoring to support black organisations and develop their partners' capacity. Ujima Housing Association in London (including Brent), mentioned earlier, is an example of a significant black-led RSL which has developed through this route.

Capacity building and sustainability are linked to the ability of new BMEOs to develop to meet new needs. There is clear evidence that many funding organisations have long-standing funding arrangements with a small number of large voluntary organis-ations, most of which are white-led.

Even where black-led organisations are concerned, the pattern is the same: a small number of long-established bodies receive the bulk of the funding. For regional, quasi-public sector agencies this is a conscious decision – it is easier for them to manage fewer contracts. For the local authorities, it is essentially a historic situation that it is difficult to change. As one senior officer in Birmingham said of transferring resources within budgets to new organisations: 'It would take member decisions.'

The result of this 'silting up' of mainstream budgets is that smaller organisations find it very difficult to access mainstream funding, have to rely on time-limited funding which is often extremely short-term, and are therefore held back in terms of growth and development.

Trusts established for grant-aid voluntary and community groups, such as the Barrow Cadbury Trust, are important in this respect. They fund a number of small and/or emerging organisations, often giving them a 'leg-up' and putting them in a position to be noticed by statutory bodies. Trusts are important providers of grants to BMEOs, although their resources are limited and they cannot be expected to provide substantial core funding year on year. (The Barrow Cadbury Trust does provide substantial, strategically targeted grant-aid which is often long term and may include core costs. However, its resources are small in comparison with need and with the resources of central and local government.)

Moving goalposts

In the course of this study it became clear that many agencies were concerned about the sustainability of funding to voluntary organisations as a result of imminent changes in funding methodologies or institutional structures. Examples of this are:

- The probation service and national accreditation – there are proposals from the Home Office which would mean standardising the programmes offered to those on probation. This could have implications for voluntary organisations, particularly smaller ones – larger national organisations such as the National Council for the Rehabilitation of Offenders, would be able to adapt.
- TECs are soon to be merged with the Further Education Funding Council to form the Local Learning and Skills Councils. The final shape of these organisations has yet to emerge. The issue of concern, as with the probation service, is whether LLSCs will

have local flexibility. Whether current initiatives will continue will, obviously, be anxiously watched by organisations currently in receipt of TEC and further education funds. Discussion with colleges of further education suggests that their work with BMEOs has already been affected by changes in the funding of colleges. Many organisations entered franchise arrangements with colleges to deliver training, thereby receiving funds directly into their budgets, but have had this method of funding cut.

• A significant amount of funding will soon be transferred from the health authority directly to locally-based primary care groups and trusts. This will mean an end to joint funding (for example, social services and health authority funding of the provision for people with a mental illness). Numerous voluntary organisations have obtained funds through such joint funding, including BMEOs such as Handsworth Community Care and the UK Asian Women's Centre. There is concern whether primary care groups and trusts will show the same level of understanding of the importance of BMEOs as social services departments and the health authorities.

Impact of area targeting

It is argued in various policy documents that area targeting provides a better basis for involving local communities and for tackling problems holistically.

Funding for regeneration initiatives has increasingly been provided on this basis. Encouraging neighbourhood management is now being raised as a necessary policy for tackling social exclusion. Has this led to better targeting of resources towards black and minority ethnic organisations and has it improved their sustainability?

Evidence collected for this study is not conclusive on whether these programmes are proving more successful in reaching BME communities or involving BMEOs than mainstream programmes. The non-neighbourhood basis of most organisations included in the survey would indicate that they may not be beneficiaries of the latest variant of area-based intervention. However, some agencies are clearly tapping into SRB funds and ensuring that community involvement is an integral part of their strategies. Guidance produced for these programmes by the regional development agencies and government offices emphasises the importance of targeting BME communities to meet their needs and of involving BMEOs as partners. But these programmes involve short-term funding and unless these funds are used to enable the development of income-generating activity by BMEOs, or the needs of BMEOs are eventually taken on by mainstream programmes, then sustainability will remain an issue.

Measuring impact

As mentioned at the start of this

chapter, there was not much evidence of rigorous monitoring or evaluation of the role BMEOs play in assisting organisations develop their objectives. Many agencies did have some method, often crude and lacking a qualitative dimension, of analysing the ultimate clients by ethnic categories. This allowed a certain level of analysis in terms of racial equality effectiveness at the point of service, but it did not enable a knowledge of which processes were effective.

This would require an analysis of the role of BMEO groups in shaping and delivering services. Indeed, where SRB has provided funding to umbrella groups (whose role is to improve processes), the monitoring methodologies were seen as an obstacle to the effective delivery of services. It was felt they focused on narrow outputs rather than on the improvement of these processes.

5. Conclusions and Policy Implications

The importance of BMEOs and the need for a policy

Inevitably, the findings from an initial exploratory study such as this will have their limitations. The researchers cannot come up with solutions to the multi-faceted challenges faced by black and minority ethnic organisations in today's climate.

However, in this chapter we attempt to draw some overarching conclusions from our study and indicate some of the policy implications which we believe flow from it. Our main conclusions and recommendations are in bold text.

On the basis of our research, there are between 5000 and 5500 black and minority ethnic organisations operating in England and Wales. They provide services directly to black and minority ethnic communities and, on the basis of our findings, we are convinced they play an important advocacy role in mediating the relationship between these communities and the mainstream agencies responsible for providing them with services.

Many BMEOs have been in existence for ten years or more and some have become a key reference point for the more disadvantaged members of the community.

On the basis of our results we conclude that BMEOs are an integral part of the infrastructure required for eliminating social exclusion and deprivation if the notion of a multi-ethnic society is to have any positive meaning.

We base these statements on the findings of our postal survey and case studies which suggest that:

* most BME organisations in England and Wales today were started by people from a particular minority ethnic group;
* the majority serve people from a particular ethnic group on a neighbourhood or town/borough basis;
* their principal users are from socially excluded groups, or from those facing social exclusion issues within black and minority communities. These include people on low incomes, benefits recipients and refugees.

Social exclusion can be defined according to the specific groups which are excluded, such as refugees, certain ethnic minority groups and travellers. Measurable targets can be set for reducing the degree of that exclusion. Current European Union development policy, for example, is built around the notion of creating 'sustainable benefits for target groups'.[39] There is no reason why this cannot be applied to groups defined as socially excluded in the UK.

Social inclusion, which is increasingly becoming the buzzword when it comes to reducing poverty in the UK, is much less easy to define and act on. The worry is that the notion of 'inclusion' will become so all-embracing – with mainstream organisations trying to ensure that gender, sexual orientation, disability and other 'diversity' issues are all covered – that the specific inclusion needs of Britain's visible minorities will become all but lost.

BMEOs, in both their advocacy and service delivery roles, are key to ensuring that the 'excluded' are 'included'. Social inclusion policies, therefore, need to have a BMEO component built in which recognises their key role in social inclusion processes and which enhances their self-help capabilities. Capacity-building programmes should concentrate on strengthening BMEOs to ensure that disadvantaged members of the minority communities are fully included in the 'inclusion' process (at least as far as services are concerned).

This policy implication flows in part from survey and case study evidence that BMEOs do constitute a specific sector within the voluntary and community sector by dint of the fact that:

- they serve particular minority ethnic communities who face their own particular issues in terms of economic and social disadvantage;

linguistic barriers and the maintenance of cultural identity; and
- they place a much greater emphasis on tackling racial inequality and injustice than the voluntary sector as a whole.

BMEOs' contribution to civil society is already recognised in government policy in, for example, the wording of the Voluntary Sector Compact. This recognition by government needs to be embedded across the whole vista of social, economic and environmental policy.

The existing Voluntary Sector Compact framework could be extended to encourage local mainstream agencies to ring-fence resources specifically for BMEO capacity building as part of their planning/consultation budgets, and as part of their service delivery budgets.

Our research suggests that the Home Office grants to strengthen black and minority ethnic infrastructure organisations, introduced in 1999, should continue and be extended.

Many of the BMEOs interviewed during the course of our research endorsed this initiative, seeing it as helping in their lobbying efforts and in providing access to additional locally based resources.

Some mainstream organisations also supported the idea, in part because of the guidance BMEO networks could give in engaging more fully with the local BME communities.

Sustainability and capacity building

A common perception of BMEOs in England and Wales is that they are generally small, living a hand-to-mouth existence, with their sustainability continually under threat.

Our research indicates that, while this may be the reality for many smaller, non-formal organisations, BMEOs have become an important factor in the voluntary sector within England and Wales. Nevertheless, although black housing associations may tend to be better funded than other BMEOs, set against white housing associations they are still relatively small in terms of funding.

Our survey and case studies suggest that BMEOs have shown, and will continue to show, more staying power than the common perception suggests.

For example, more than 60 per cent had been in existence for more than ten years, most had a formal legal status, a significant proportion owned their own premises, and demand for at least some BMEO services remained high.

The social exclusion and lack of access to mainstream resources experienced by Britain's BME communities have forced BMEOs to play a direct role in:

- providing access to public services – especially where race, culture or language barriers are significant impediments;
- creating strategic alliances and partnerships with mainstream agencies unfamiliar with BME needs;
- educating the wider community on issues connected with the notion of a multicultural society;
- developing BME board members, workers and administrators, who might otherwise have had little opportunity to gain such experience; and
- contributing to the local development planning of some of Britain's most deprived areas.

Nevertheless, many BMEOs have to devote a great deal of time and effort in struggling to survive. This detracts from their ability to provide the services they were established to deliver.

Reinforcing sustainability has to be a fundamental part of any policy for strengthening BMEOs.

Our results suggest the following as being key factors contributing to sustainability:

- recognising the importance of core funding to sustaining organisations;
- encouraging these organisations to build up a capital asset base and to develop income-generating activities, combined with the necessary training;
- providing capacity-building support related to the services (including advocacy) that the minority ethnic organisations intend to provide; the

physical, financial and human resources that they will be managing; and their ability to develop and respond to the changing external environment; and

- providing on-the-ground, continuous development and mentoring support in combination with funding support.

Furthermore, encouraging 'investment in the community' is an obvious way of building up both the sustainability of BME communities and the BMEOs themselves. A number of housing associations, including black ones, are exploring the concept of 'social investment' as a way of bringing together at local level the key partners needed to help address the building of sustainable communities.

An example of this is the Handsworth Area Regeneration Trust (HART) initiative in Handsworth, Birmingham. This originally involved five housing associations coming together to see how they could deliver better services and housing developments in the area. It has now widened to include other agencies, such as the local authority, and has won Single Regeneration Budget funding.

Our working definition of capacity building highlights the connection between BMEO sustainability and the sustainability of BME communities as a whole. It also emphasises the importance of linking capacity building to the specific functions of any BMEO.

The emphasis will be on the development of particular institutions, their human

and material resources, their organisational management and their administrative capacities...More specifically the aim is to improve significantly the outputs and impacts.[40]

A key area of capacity building identified in our study is increasing the ability of BMEOs to participate meaningfully in partnerships. This is a question both of building the capacity of BMEOs and the capacity of mainstream agencies to work most productively with BMEOs.

Capacity building of BMEOs, we would argue, is an essential ingredient of capacity building of the minority ethnic communities as a whole.

Building capacity, however, is one thing. Funding is another. To quote a BMEO from one of our case studies:

It's no good building my capacity if I ain't got no money to run the thing.

Mentoring

A number of mainstream agencies contacted during the study suggested that one of their key roles with respect to BME communities was, in effect, to act as mentors of BMEOs, introducing them to potential mainstream partners and helping broker alliances with the wider community.

In addition, they were able to exert pressure on mainstream organisations to take BMEOs into account and were also able to provide the BMEOs with support and advice on meeting the expectations and standards of the mainstream organisations.

It was apparent, however, that most of this mentoring was on an informal and ad hoc basis. It often depended on the efforts of one or two key individuals who were personally committed to 'championing the cause'. Such individuals could, if suitably empowered within their own organisations, play a much greater role in brokering alliances between BMEOs and the wider community.

Relying on a handful of individuals to drive forward BMEO support through government departments and agencies is a fragile policy base. A positive move would be the establishment of a network of BMEO mentors by the Home Office, which could act as an agent of change throughout public and voluntary institutions.

'Joined-up' policy and practice

The picture that emerged from our case studies was a mixture of inconsistent policies towards local BMEOs. Some mainstream organisations based their funding on contracts and left the issues of core funding, capacity building and the ability of a BMEO to bid for these contracts, to other organisations or partnerships. (Occasionally they funded these other organisations fairly generously to provide capacity building.)

There were also examples of duplication of capacity-building programmes and consultation arrangements. Even

where there were excellent examples of networking between front-line workers from different mainstream organisations, these did not take place within agreed strategic frameworks, but rather reflected the exigencies of daily life.

What is needed is far more strategic coordination of support to BMEOs at appropriate geographical levels, to ensure that they receive funding packages which improve their long-term sustainability and the quality of services they can provide.

For example, a specific BMEO might be recognised as being of critical importance by a number of mainstream organisations. Each of these organisations could agree to supply part of a comprehensive package of support – core funding, training, support to purchase certain assets, volunteer support, output-driven contracts and so on – in the knowledge that other partners will supply other necessary components of the package.

This is already done on an ad hoc basis with some BMEOs, but not consistently across the whole sector.

The role of BMEOs in any areas of joined-up area strategies should be recognised and clearly defined, so that they too can approach issues and their target groups more holistically.

Our survey suggested that many of these organisations are already providing services and advocacy across a range of policy areas and could therefore provide a good foundation for developing a more joined-up approach.

This 'breaking down of the silos' is recognised as a policy objective by government departments in tackling social exclusion. It now needs to be reflected in policy and practice towards BMEOs (and the voluntary/community sector more generally) at a regional and more local level.

This wind of change in public policy will require more than the development of a Voluntary Sector Compact with a BMEO component by one government department, useful though that is. It will require a review of policy and practice by each wing of central, regional and local government, by quasi-public agencies and by large voluntary organisations, which examines their overall impact on social exclusion and racial equality.

Targeting communities

A BMEO support policy needs to recognise that local circumstances differ and that these differences are usually reflected in the local structure of the BMEO sector. Consultation arrangements and support to BMEOs who are directly delivering services are most effective when they are based on an understanding of local situations.

Responsiveness to local differences is helped by having, and listening to, local 'patch' workers and by employing BME staff.

Our survey suggests that BMEOs provide services mainly for the local (neighbourhood or town/borough) community. 'Hard' services (those relating directly to health, leisure and day care facilities, nurseries, benefits advice, translation services and so forth) are the ones most likely to be in demand.

The long-term sustainability of BMEOs will depend on the extent to which resources are made directly available to them, so that they can continue to provide these kinds of service to the immediate community. The extent to which 'neighbourhood targeting' forms part of the government's strategy for dealing with social exclusion and deprivation will therefore be of prime importance to BMEO survival.

Neighbourhood targeting and management are likely to play an increasing role in government thinking. Guidance for recent initiatives recommends the prioritisation of areas with significant black and minority ethnic populations.

BMEOs with a well established local base will need, therefore, to become increasingly involved in alliances and partnerships with non-BMEO bodies.

A key issue will revolve around the allocation of resources via these alliances, with BMEOs demanding the resources which will allow them to play a significant role.

Flexibility will need to be exercised in drawing in BMEOs into area targeted initiatives.

Although BMEOs tend to focus their activities on specific localities reflecting neighbourhood concentrations of BME residents, our survey suggests that these localities will tend to be larger than some of the areas currently targeted.

The importance of religious organisations

The brief for this study explicitly excluded surveying the details of support provided by religious organisations (see Chapter 1 for details). However, our research confirmed the experience of people working in BME communities, namely that religious organisations play a key (but not exclusive) role in delivering material, as well as spiritual, services to these communities.

Black and minority ethnic religious organisations are often bypassed by grant regimes which exclude support for the promotion of specific religions. They tend not to be as skilled as white-led religious organisations in demonstrating a separation between religious activity and secular community activity. (Some would say that there is no essential division between the religious and community activities of these religious organisations.)

We recommend that grant programmes need to be operated with sufficient flexibility if the important role BME religious organisations play in BME communities' secular life is to be supported.

Monitoring

Public, private and voluntary sector partnerships have become essential in underpinning strategies aimed at combating urban deprivation and social exclusion – particularly the Single Regeneration Budget. Many do, in fact, incorporate indicators of ethnic minority benefit as output measures, and several partnership programmes in our case studies had BME community needs at the core of their objectives.

What is not being monitored, however, is the extent to which BMEOs are significantly involved in these partnerships, whether in a decision-making or service-delivery capacity. Nor, with particular reference to sustainability, whether such involvement generates any organisational revenue. The reason for this is that there are no mechanisms in place by which such monitoring could be carried out.

In addition, output monitoring by BME umbrella support organisations funded by partnership programmes did not reflect the strategic outcomes being aimed at, and were a hindrance to the achievement of these aims.

It may well be that some partnerships are able to achieve their BME community output targets without the specific involvement of BMEOs (the researchers had no access to relevant data). Even so, there is a case for BMEOs being involved in such partnerships, in order to benefit from 'technology transfer' as they learn to meet community needs.

We recommend that programmes that include aims of delivering benefits to BME communities should be monitored for the achievement of these aims. They should include qualitative indicators of whether these benefits are likely to be sustainable.

'Incubating' the next generation

The demography and needs of BME communities in England and Wales are changing, and new BMEOs and new projects by existing organisations are appearing. These are often supported by national grants programmes (such as the National Lottery Charities Board) and by specific, short-term initiatives (such as SRB programmes). However, BMEOs thus supported may have real difficulties in accessing mainstream funds once the short-term funding runs out.

Mainstream agencies have to find ways of helping innovative projects, which are already succeeding in meeting priority needs, to 'graduate' into more long-term, mainstream funding and support. This includes policies to 'incubate' these projects, such as providing shared premises, mentoring support from more established BMEOs, help in making contacts and championing the initiatives in partnership forums.

Many of the older, more established organisations already own their own properties, occasionally on a joint basis. These have often been renovated and refurbished to meet the needs of beneficiaries. They appear to have little interest in shared facilities which involve:

> *paying rent, so that someone else can own property in our communities while we finance it.*

This feeling has been exacerbated by what are seen as attempts by local authorities to force through organisational mergers, by supporting only organisations which base themselves in council-sponsored sites.

On the other hand, less well-established and smaller organisations felt that sharing administrative staff, office equipment and workspace facilities could be to their advantage. (For example, jointly occupied centres could be used to offer day care and nursery provision; seminar and meeting facilities; and/or could provide high quality administrative backup, such as book-keeping support, help with tendering for contracts, or computer support services etc.)

Findings from the postal survey indicate that this is already happening in some parts of the country, sometimes under the auspices of older BMEOs who have accommodated the newer groups in their own premises.

Future scenarios

The trends we identified in our interviews suggest two contrasting, potential future scenarios for support to BMEOs.

Scenario 1

The first involves a danger of a continued, non-strategic, non-joined-up approach, with a growing emphasis on an output-driven, 'contract culture'. This seeks to deliver equality outputs which will offer opportunities to all, regardless of ethnic background, without due regard to nurturing the sustainability of one of the prime mechanisms for delivering these outputs, the BMEO sector.

This danger will be increased by the shake-up in institutional arrangements for the delivery of much of public policy – the creation of primary care groups and trusts in the NHS and the Learning and Skills Councils, for example. It risks losing the lessons learnt and the local knowledge of key individuals who have grasped the opportunities provided by policy to offer direct support to BMEOs.

The danger will further be reinforced by non-black-led organisations winning resources to deliver services to black and minority ethnic communities at the expense of BMEOs. In this scenario, BMEOs survive, but with increasing difficulty, providing poorer quality services and having less and less influence on mainstream policies.

Scenario 2

The second scenario is more optimistic, with:

- individual agencies and arms of government conducting in-depth reviews of their own policies with a view to incorporating effective, enabling policies towards the BMEO sector;
- growing strategic approaches and partnerships which recognise the need for sustainable BMEOs to deliver initiatives which tackle social exclusion; and
- a BMEO sector with growing confidence and capabilities, providing continually improving services, helping make mainstream service providers' delivery more sensitive and effective, and adapting to the changing needs of the communities they were set up to serve.

There are embryonic examples of this second approach in some SRB partnerships which have been funded in the West Midlands. One is 'Birmingham CAN' (Action for Social Inclusion: Birmingham Community Action Network), an SRB-funded partnership led by the Birmingham Voluntary Sector Council to encourage initiatives which counter social exclusion. The other is the Black Minority Ethnic Consortium SRB5 partnership in Wolverhampton.

Conclusion

Black and minority ethnic communities continue to face deprivation, social exclusion and discrimination to a greater extent than most other communities in England and Wales. Mainstream organisations are failing to tackle these issues adequately.

This has been recognised in the Stephen Lawrence Inquiry and in the emerging government policies on social exclusion and neighbourhood renewal.

However, if this recognition is to lead to effective policy and practice – and to real change – then measures to support and sustain black and minority ethnic volun-tary organisations need to be given a much more prominent and central role.

These measures need to be implemented in a coordinated, strategic and long-term way. But they have to recognise the very diverse characteristics of the various BMEOs, as highlighted in this report.

It would be better to encourage agencies to develop their own services, and to introduce measures to ensure their sustainability, rather than continuing with the current fragmented and contract-driven arrangements.

The alternative is the persistence of a vicious circle of social exclusion for black and minority ethnic communities.

Appendix I
Black and Minority Ethnic Organisations Interviewed

1   Age Concern, Brent
2   Asian Resource Centre, Birmingham
3   ACAFES, Birmingham
4   Afro-Caribbean People's Movement, Birmingham
5   Afro-Caribbean Resource Centre, Birmingham
6   Asian Stroke Victim Support, Birmingham
7   Birmingham Partnership for Change
8   Birmingham Race Action Partnership
9   Black Regeneration Forum
10 Black Regeneration Network, Birmingham
11 Black Women's Mental Health Project, Brent
12 Brent African and Caribbean Disabled People
13 Brent Community Housing
14 Brent Indian Association
15 Brent Youth Justice Team
16 Black Training and Enterprise Group
17 Council of Ethnic Minority Voluntary Organisations
18 Council of Sikh Gurdwaras, Birmingham
19 Handsworth Community Care, Birmingham
20 Harambee Organisation, Birmingham
21 Hindu Council, Brent
22 Sacara Fashion and Training Centre, Brent
23 Sickle Cell Society, Birmingham
24 Sickle Cell Society, Brent
25 Euddenhill Community Centre, Brent
26 Project Fullemploy
27 Marcus Garvey Day Nursery, Birmingham
28 PATH
29 Pubbs Road Community Centre, Brent
30 Tamil Centre, Brent
31 Ting-A-Ling, Birmingham
32 Ujala/British Muslim Women Welfare Association
33 UK Asian Women's Centre, Birmingham
34 Stonebridge Park Centre, Brent

Mainstream Agencies Interviewed

1   Advantage West Midlands
2   Barrow Cadbury Trust
3   Birmingham City Council – Economic Development
4   Birmingham City Council – Education
5   Birmingham City Council – Equal Opportunities
6   Birmingham City Council – Housing
7   Birmingham City Council – Policy Unit
8   Birmingham City Council – Recreation and Leisure – Leisure Division
9   Birmingham City Council – Recreation and Leisure – Youth Division
10   Birmingham City Council – Social Services
11   Birmingham Core Skills Partnership
12   Birmingham Health Authority
13   Birmingham and Solihull TEC – Access Division
14   Birmingham and Solihull TEC – Business Development
15   Birmingham Voluntary Sector Council
16   Brent Council – Community Unit
17   Brent Council – Economic Development
18   Brent Council – Education
19   Brent Council – Housing
20   Brent Youth Justice Team
21   Business Link, Brent
22   City College, Birmingham
23   Employment Service, Birmingham
24   Focus Housing
25   Government Office for London
26   Government Office for the West Midlands
27   HAMAC
28   Handsworth Area Regeneration Trust
29   Home Office
30   Housing Corporation, West Midlands
31   National Lottery Charities Board
32   Network Housing, Brent
33   Notting Hill Housing Trust

34   PATH West Midlands
35   West Midlands Probation Service
36   Scarman Trust, Birmingham
37   Saltley and Small Heath SRB
38   Sparkbrook SRB
39   Wembley Park SRB

Assessing the Number of BME Voluntary Organisations in England and Wales

Methodology

The first stage of the project was concerned with creating a sampling frame for the postal survey, achieved by obtaining directories and lists of BME voluntary organisations which had been created by libraries, local authorities and other information providers.

The lists derived from these sources were carefully scanned, to ensure that (as far as possible) questionnaires were sent out only to BME organisations. This yielded more than 3600 addresses. This exercise covered the main geographical areas in which the minority ethnic group population is concentrated. It should, therefore, have identified a large percentage of all the BME voluntary organisations present in England and Wales.

The postal survey yielded responses from about 200 BME voluntary organisations across England and Wales (from over 1100 who were sent questionnaires). This probably represents no more than 5 per cent of all the BME voluntary organisations in existence.

Unfortunately, the sources used to derive lists of BME voluntary organisations vary considerably in their coverage, and tend to be least comprehensive in some of the areas of greatest minority ethnic group concentration (such as some London boroughs). It was thus judged necessary to use statistical techniques in order to estimate the number of BME voluntary organisations from the information available.

The approach taken is to estimate the number of organisations which should exist in each of the 403 local authority districts, and sum the total of these estimates across England and Wales. It is assumed that the number of organisations in an area is a function of the number of people from minority ethnic groups resident in a given area, since demand for their services will be greater the larger the minority population.

Figure 10 shows that the greater the minority population, the larger the number of organisations. However, there is some variability, with a number of districts with large minority populations containing small numbers of BME voluntary organisations. One implication of this is that there is a high degree of uncertainty about the true number of BME voluntary organisations in those districts with small numbers of organisations. In order to improve the accuracy

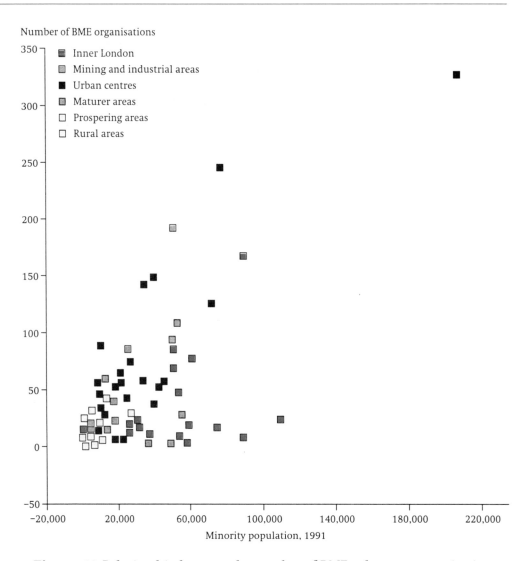

Number of BME organisations

Legend:
- ▣ Inner London
- ▢ Mining and industrial areas
- ■ Urban centres
- ▨ Maturer areas
- □ Prospering areas
- □ Rural areas

Minority population, 1991

Figure 10 *Relationship between the number of BME voluntary organisations and the minority population in 1991*

of the regression model, three London boroughs (Brent, Ealing and Lambeth), in which the list of voluntary organisations was known to be deficient, were excluded from the estimate.

The scatter diagram in Figure 10 (which makes use of an ONS classification of local authority districts

into six 'families' of areas with similar socio-economic characteristics) reveals that there appear to be fewer BME voluntary organisations per minority person in London boroughs than in districts located outside the capital. This might be because the greater concentration of people in London enables organisations

Table 16 *Regression coefficients*

	Unstandardised coefficients	Standard error	Standardised coefficients	t-statistic
(Constant)	2.150573	2.030987		1.058881
Minority population in London boroughs	0.000893	0.000106	0.339116	8.388848
Minority population in other districts	0.001873	8.93E−05	0.847579	20.96693

located in the capital to serve larger numbers of people than those located outside, which may face a more dispersed population, with the need for more locally-based organisations. Accordingly, the model included separate population variables for London and elsewhere.

The regression coefficients measuring the relationship between minority population and number of BME voluntary organisations are presented in Table 16. The model finally chosen accounted for three-quarters of the variance in the data (an R^2 adjusted for the number of explanatory variables of 0.737 – a very high degree of explanation for data of this type). Its 'fit' to the data was statistically highly significant, though the associated standard error of

the model was 22.2 (the range of uncertainty above and below the estimated number of organisations for a local authority). The coefficients on the two population variables were positive and highly statistically significant.

The model reveals that the number of BME voluntary organisations increases with increasing minority population at a faster rate outside London than in London.

These parameters were then multiplied against population data for each of the 403 local authority districts in England and Wales, and the estimated number of organisations in each obtained. Summing these local estimates yields an estimate of 5077 BME voluntary organisations in England and Wales.

Notes and References

1   Modood, T, Berthoud, R and others (1997) *Ethnic Minorities in Britain: Diversity and Disadvantage.* London: Policy Studies Institute

2   CRE (1997) 'Employment and Unemployment', Factsheet. London: Commission for Racial Equality

3   See for example, Owen, D (1993) 'Ethnic Minorities in Great Britain: Housing and Family Characteristics', NEMDA 1991 Census Statistical Paper No 4. Coventry: University of Warwick Centre for Research in Ethnic Relations, and Mason, D (1995) *Race and Ethnicity in Modern Britain.* Oxford: Oxford University Press

4   Chahal, K (1999) 'Ethnic diversity, neighbourhoods and housing', Foundations Paper. York: Joseph Rowntree Foundation

5   Berthoud, R (1998) *The Incomes of Ethnic Minorities.* Institute for Social and Economic Research report 98-1. Colchester: University of Essex

6   Crook, J (1995) *Invisible Partners: The Impact of the SRB on Black Communities.* London: NCVO – Voice of the Voluntary Sector

7   Lattimer, M (1991) *Funding Black Groups: A Report into the Charitable Funding of Ethnic Minority Organisations.* Directory of Social Change/Urban Trust, and CAF (1999) *Patterns in Charitable Trust and Foundation Funding of Black and Minority Ethnic Beneficiaries in the UK.* Charities Aid Foundation

8   NCVO (1996) *Meeting the Challenge of Change: Voluntary Action into the 21st Century.* London: NCVO – Voice of the Voluntary Sector

9   SIA (1998) *The Black Voluntary Sector and the Compact: An Executive Summary of the SIA Consultations Seminars.* SIA – The National Development Agency for the Black Voluntary Sector

10   See Marshall, T (1996) 'Can we define the voluntary sector?' in Billis, D and Harris, M (eds) *Voluntary Agencies, Challenges of Organisation and Management.* Basingstoke: Macmillan

11   Salamon, L and Anheier, H (1997) *Defining the Nonprofit Sector: A Cross-national Analysis.* Manchester: Manchester University Press

12   See Marshall, T (1996) 'Can we define the voluntary sector?' in Billis, D and Harris, M (eds) *Voluntary Agencies, Challenges of Organisation and Management.* Basingstoke: Macmillan

13   A similar situation applies to the Chinese community in Britain, although its origins go back slightly further

14   IRR (1993) *Community Care: The Black Experience.* London: Institute of Race Relations

15   Sivanandan, A (1982) *A Different Hunger: Writings on Black Resistance.* London: Institute of Race Relations

16   IRR (1993) *Community Care: The Black Experience.* London: Institute of Race Relations

17   Rex, J (1991) *Ethnic Identity and Ethnic Mobilization in Britain,* Monographs in Ethnic Relations No 5. ESRC/Centre for Research in Ethnic Relations, 1991

18   Department of Education (1991) *The Education of Immigrants.* Education Survey 13. London: HMSO

19   Through fitting a regression relationship between the minority share of the population and the number of minority organisations, the details of the statistical analysis are available in Appendix III to this report

20   See, for example, Peach, C (1996) 'Does Britain have ghettoes?', Transactions of the Institute of British Geographers, NS, 21, 216–235; and Ratcliffe, P (ed) *Ethnicity in the 1991 Census vol 3 – Social Geography and Ethnicity in Britain: Geographical Spread, Spatial Concentration and Internal Migration*. London: HMSO

21   See, for example, Chahal, K (1999) 'Ethnic diversity, neighbourhoods and housing', Foundations Paper. York: Joseph Rowntree Foundation

22   Organisations could choose more than one status; for example, many were both 'charities' and 'companies limited by guarantee'

23   Home Office (1999) *Strengthening the Black and Minority Ethnic Voluntary Sector Infrastructure*. London: Home Office Active Community Unit

24   Questionnaire responses indicate that BMEOs established on the basis of shared interest were less likely to be formally run

25   The important exception was religious groups, which we had been asked not to include in the study. We are now of the opinion that future work in this area should include these groups as a matter of course

26   See McGlone, F et al (1998) *Families and Kinship*. London: Family Policy Studies Centre

27   Voluntary Action Research (1992) *Encouraging Signs? A Report on a Survey of Black Participation in Voluntary Organisations*. Paper No 5, National Coalition for Black Volunteering/Volunteer Centre

28   Chahal, K (1999) 'Ethnic diversity, neighbourhoods and housing', Foundations Paper. York: Joseph Rowntree Foundation

29   Chahal, K (1999) 'Ethnic diversity, neighbourhoods and housing', Foundations Paper. York: Joseph Rowntree Foundation

30   du Boulay, D (1995) *Black Voluntary Sector: Mapping Exercise*. West Midlands Regional Training Group

31   Francique, M (1999) *Volunteering from a Black Perspective*. Black Information Link, http://www.blink.org.uk/reports2/blackvolu.htm

32   Black Perspectives on Volunteering Group (1993) *Black People and Volunteering*, Advance

33   Lisk, F (1996) 'Capacity building for management and development', *The Courier*, No 159 Sep–Oct

34   NCVO (1996) *Meeting the Challenge of Change – Voluntary Action into the 21st Century*. Commission on the Future of the Voluntary Sector. London: NCVO

35   Burridge, D (1996) *What Local Groups Need*. London: NCVO

36   This aims to set the tone for relations between all arms of central and local government and the voluntary sector. The Compact specifically recognises the role of the BMEO sector and therefore also aims to influence positively policy towards this sector

37   These are sometimes awarded through departments (as in Birmingham) and sometimes through a corporate voluntary/community sector unit (as in Brent. Birmingham has a central grants budget as well as departmental ones, but this is being transferred to neighbourhood offices). There is an interesting debate as to which method allows the best strategic and sustainability support. On the one hand, a corporate unit allows a 'joining-up' of policies and provision of consistent capacity building support. On the other hand, support and capacity building may be most effective when delivered in the context of a specific policy area

38   This interviewee suggested that all grants should have a 'per cent for capacity' rather like the 'per cent for art' initiative in publicly funded building projects

39 Project cycle management (integrated approach and logical framework) DG VII European Commission

40 Lisk, F (1996) 'Capacity building for management and development', *The Courier*, No 159 Sep–Oct